# CRAVE
## SAN FRANCISCO

*The Urban Girl's Manifesto*

Melody Biringer

1st Edition

**Crave San Francisco: The Urban Girl's Manifesto**
A publication of Crave Party ©
1805-12th Ave W #A, Seattle, WA 98119
Ring: 206-282-0713
Email: crave@craveparty.com
www.craveparty.com

While every effort was made to ensure the accuracy of the information, details are
subject to change, so please call ahead. Neither Crave Party, Crave San Francisco
or the publisher shall be responsible for any consequences arising from the publication or use.

All of the editorial in this publication is the sole opinion of Crave San Francisco:
The Urban Girl's Manifesto, and our contributing writers. No fees or services were
rendered in exchange for inclusion in this publication.

Copy Edited by Jennifer Worick
Printing consultation & Design by Kaie Wellman, Cabazon Studio, Portland, OR
Design by Susan Barnes, Susan Barnes Design, Seattle, WA

Maps are not to scale.

ISBN 0-9670213-3-1
First Edition November 2006

## PRINTED IN SINGAPORE

# Contents

## Welcome to Crave San Francisco

**CRAVE San Francisco is more than a guidebook.**

It's about more than where-to-go and what-to-do. It's full of more than basic information. CRAVE San Francisco is a savvy, quality-of-lifestyle book devoted entirely to the best local businesses owned or managed by women. Featuring 220 spots in 10 of San Francisco's favorite neighborhoods, CRAVE San Francisco will direct you to top boutiques, spas, cafés, candy shops, yoga studios and more and introduce you to the inspired, dedicated women behind these exceptional enterprises. At these spots creativity, quality and customer service are paramount. Not only is CRAVE San Francisco an intelligent guidebook for those wanting to know what's happening throughout town, it's also a guidebook for those who recognize and value the contributions that spirited business women make to our city.

# The Urban Girl's Manifesto

## WE CRAVE COMMUNITY

At CRAVE San Francisco we believe in acknowledging, celebrating and passionately supporting locally owned businesses. We know that when encouraged to thrive, neighborhood establishments enhance communities. These spots are original and quirky and provide rich experiences not usually encountered in mass-market chains. At CRAVE San Francisco we also know that savvy women are interested in more than mindlessly spending money on shoes, facials and sweet treats, so we've included the profiles of 40 local business women to educate and inspire your own inner entrepreneur.

## WE CRAVE ADVENTURE

We could all use a getaway, and at CRAVE San Francisco we believe that you don't need to be a jetsetter to have a little adventure. There's so much to explore right here. We encourage you to break your routine, to venture from your regular haunts, to visit new neighborhoods, to explore all the funky finds and surprising spots that our splendid city has to offer. Whether it's to hunt for a birthday gift, indulge in a spa treatment, order a bouquet of flowers or sip happy hour cocktails with the girls after work, let CRAVE San Francisco be your map for a one-of-a-kind, custom hometown journey.

## WE CRAVE QUALITY

At CRAVE San Francisco we know that a satisfying shopping trip requires more than a simple exchange of money for goods, and that a rejuvenating spa date entails more than a quick clip of the cuticles and a swipe of polish. We know that you value quality and thoughtful service. We know you want to come away with more than a new dress or a French manicure. You want to come away feeling uplifting, feeling beautiful, feeling excited, feeling relaxed and relieved knowing you got the most bang for your buck. We have scoured the city so that you will never to be disappointed. In CRAVE San Francisco you will find hidden gems and old standbys all with one thing in common: they are the best of the best.

# THE HAIGHT

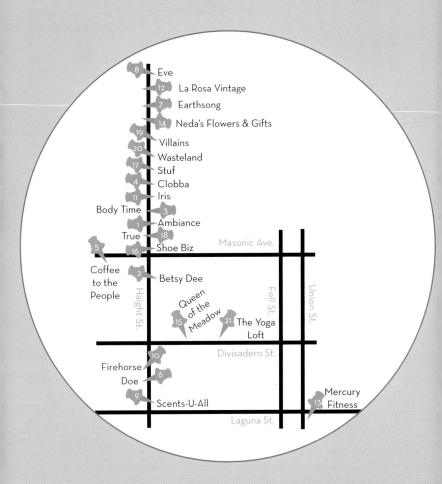

8  Eve
12  La Rosa Vintage
7  Earthsong
14  Neda's Flowers & Gifts
19  Villains
20  Wasteland
17  Stuf
4  Clobba
11  Iris
Body Time
3
1  Ambiance
True
18
5  Shoe Biz
16
Coffee to the People
2  Betsy Dee
Masonic Ave.
Haight St.
Fell St.
Union St.
Queen of the Meadow
15
21  The Yoga Loft
Divisadero St.
10
Firehorse
6
Doe
9  Scents-U-All
Mercury Fitness
13
Laguna St.

1. Ambiance  2. betsy dee/sf

3. Body Time  4. Clobba  5. Coffee to the People  6. Doe

7. Earthsong  8. Eve  9. Feel More Scents U All

10. firehorse  11. Iris  12. La Rosa Vintage Boutique

13. Mercury Fitness  14. Neda's Flowers & Gifts  15. Queen of the Meadow

16. Shoe Biz  17. Stuf  18. True  19. Villains, Villains Vault, Villains Shoes

20. Wasteland  21. The Yoga Loft

*Forget the tie-dye -- hippies & hipsters unite while perusing this '60's retro walk down memory lane. Soak in the sights and sounds of another era while taking in some of the most exclusive boutiques & vintage clothing shops in town.*

### 1. Ambiance

1458 Haight St.  415-552-5095 (boutique)
www.ambiancesf.com - Owner: Donna Leary
If you're looking bring romance to your shopping experience, you've come to the right place. Shop for vintage-inspired dresses, hip separates, killer party dresses, and the absolute best shoes and accessories under chandeliers and amidst vintage tchotchkes and deco furniture. Ambiance is a dream store for the girls.

### 2. betsy dee/sf

1322 Haight St.  415-861-2527 (boutique)
Owner: Betsy Dee
"Global style, local talent." That's the credo at betsy dee/sf, where you'll find affordable chic with an urban twist, from both established and emerging California designers.

### 3. Body Time

1465 Haight St. 415-551-1070  (pamper)
www.bodytime.com - Owner: Manda Heron
Create a unique fragrance at the Bay Area's original body shop. Choose a scent from 80 perfume and essential oils, from Pikake to bestseller China Rain, and then add your custom blend to any body product. If you want to treat your skin, Body Time's Botanicals line contains nurturing, natural ingredients. Whatever your body needs, Body Time is the place to go.

### 4. Clobba

1604 Haight St.  415-864-4701 (boutique)
Manager: Sabrina Chargualaf
This three-level shop is geared toward the trendy carrying edgy yet affordable designs for men and women, with labels mainly from Los Angeles and New York. Look for their scandalously cheap sales racks with items for less than $15 in the back Clobba's accomodating staff is knowledgeable about the clothes and accessories they're selling.

## Susan Jones

QUEEN OF THE MEADOW

351 Divisadero St.
415-355-1051

"I worked in the mental health field for 10 years at a psychiatric unit of a hospital, initially working on both adolescent and adult in-patient units and then doing psychiatric evaluations in the emergency room. I'd always had an interest in fashion, and after 10 years in a professional environment I was ready for a creative outlet."

### INSPIRATION/MOTIVATION FOR STARTING MY BUSINESS:

I was in London in 1988 and the fashion was great- all the little shops at Hyper Hyper, Kings Road, and Camden. I loved it. I decided while I was there that I wanted to open a store. As soon as I got home I did. I wanted to bring London style to San Francisco.

### MY ROLE MODEL:

Cher! The original fashion icon. She had her own individual style, started trends, experimented with fashion – always pushed the envelope and never cared what anybody else thought. Fashion, music, film. She's done it all with style and a sense of humor and after some ups and downs she's still on top and fabulous.

### ADVICE I WOULD GIVE TO WOMEN STARTING THEIR OWN BUSINESS:

It's not as easy as it looks and it's not a hobby. Expect to work harder and longer hours than you ever have before.

### PEOPLE WOULD BE SURPRISED THAT I...

I love country music.

### PERSONAL TIME OFF INDULGENCE:

I like to be near the water – the beach, lakes, on a boat. I find the water tranquil. It's where I relax... And I like to entertain at home. It's more casual and intimate. Usually champagne or cocktails – with appetizers or dinner (always prepared by my husband. I don't cook!)

### FAVORITE GUILTY PLEASURE SHOPPING:

Riley James and Nicolette.

### MY BESTSELLERS:

Edgy and unusual styles. Anything that's unique. Currently it's super skinny leg jeans and high-waisted jeans.

## June Kim

EVE

1780 Haight St.
415-751-7720

"Be prepared to work 7 days a week. Start small (and expand later) — you will learn a lot doing it."

**INSPIRATION/MOTIVATION FOR STARTING MY BUSINESS:**
To make money!

**HOW MUCH MONEY DID IT TAKE TO START?**
A lot – more than down payment for a house.

**MY ROLE MODEL/MENTOR:**
My mother, she was a business owner herself. I grew up seeing her working with guys all the time. [Without her] I never would've dreamt of being a business owner when I was child.

**MISTAKE THAT I HOPE NOT TO REPEAT?**
Chasing shoplifters out to the street!

**WHAT I LIKE MOST ABOUT OWNING A BUSINESS:**
Being a boss, even though I'm not bossy enough.

**WHAT I LIKE LEAST ABOUT OWNING A BUSINESS:**
Responsibility for every single decision I make.

**PEOPLE WOULD BE SURPRISED THAT I...**
I'm in my 30s and own my business – most people think I'm in my early 20s, or even 18!

**FAVORITE GUILTY PLEASURE SHOPPING PLACE:**
Flika on Fillmore – they carry Scandinavian stuff.

**PERSONAL TIME OFF INDULGENCE:**
Meet my friends and talk it up, or have very nice meal to release my stress.

## 5. Coffee to the People

1206 Masonic Ave.   415-626-2435 (eats)
www.coffeetothepeople.com
Owner/Manager: Megan Harkins
A must-stop for any visit to the Haight, this
family-owned coffeehouse revives 1960s ideals.
Grab a comfy chair under the skylight and a mug
of fair trade, organic coffee or a pot of organic
tea. Vegan goodies and huge, fresh sandwiches
abound. Browse the hippie library, surf the free
wi-fi, or just soak up the atmosphere and enjoy
the people-watching.

## 6. Doe

529A Haight St.   415-558-8588 (boutique)
www.doe-sf.com - Owner: Kati Kim
An outpost for fine goods on Lower Haight, Doe
is a miniature department store that collaborates
with local and California artists, and also carries
an array of U.S., European, and Japanese designers. Doe is an urban store, with an appreciation
for nature. Informal, but with a taste for luxury,
it's a modern-day mercantile, with a minimal yet
inviting design.

## 7. Earthsong

1701 Haight St.   415-751-0127 (décor)
Owner: Robin Fett
Put the joy back into shopping! Earthsong
features an eclectic array of gorgeous hand-
embroidered, beaded, and printed clothing,
handbags, shoes, silver jewelry, and scarves. Snap
up hand-embellished items such as jewelry boxes,
pictures frames, and journals, as well as natural
candles and windchimes. Earthsong also carries
handmade home decor items like curtains, lamps,
cushion covers, bedspreads, and table decor.

## 8. Eve

1780 Haight St.   415-751-7720 (boutique)
Owner: June Kim
Looking for electric style? Look no further than
Eve, a Haight Asbury boutique that's been the
one-stop shop for fashionistas for more than six
years. The store expanded two years ago, and expanded its selection of merchandise. Eve carries
a variety of young contemporary designer clothes,
accessories, and shoes.

## 9. Feel More Scents U All

438 Haight St.  415-861-6457 (scents)
www.scentsuall.com - Owner: Lynne Elman
Frantically looking for a scent you cannot find anywhere except for that last precious drop in the bottle on your dresser? Scent completes a style, it's that finishing touch. With resins, fruits, leaves, spices, woods, and so forth, Scents U All offers a tapestry of natural personalized adornment. Call for an appointment to create a custom-blended perfume.

## 10. firehorse

659 Haight St.  415-336-0779 (pamper)
www.firehorse.com - Owner: Tracey Fischer
Uptown Lower Haight's Firehorse hair salon specializes in color and sexy haircuts in a modern minimalist design space. Have your locks rocked by any of these experienced hair artists. Get high-end results without the downtown attitude at this true neighborhood hotspot.

## 11. Iris

1472 Haight St.  415-252-1108 (lingerie)
www.irisonhaight.com - Owner: Janelle Sinclair
Set among the bead shops and tattoo parlors on Haight Street sits Iris. The periwinkle interior offers a soft yet intimate backdrop for the beautiful lines of lingerie the shop carries. Instead of your typical department store lingerie, discover a wide array of unique and fun (but still practical) undergarments.

## 12. La Rosa Vintage Boutique

1711 Haight St.  415-668-3744 (boutique)
District Manager: Rochelle Baker
A venerable institution at age 30, La Rosa is an enclave of quality vintage fashion in the counter fashion Haight-Asbury. The boutique carries the best of the bygone eras—women's and men's clothing, accessories, and jewelry from the 1880s-1970 with an emphasis on the 30s, 40s, 50s, and 60s. There is sure to be something for everyone!

Ambiance

betsy dee/sf

Body Time

Eve

Coffee to the People

Iris

## Kinda
DOE

629A Haight St.
415-558-8588  www.doe-sf.com

The owners, James and Kati Kim, opened the store on May 23, 2004, along with their first employee, Kinda, who is the manager of doe. It was a dream of the owners to open a store with their unique vision: to give local and California artists and designers a place to showcase their goods and artistic works.

**INSPIRATION/MOTIVATION TO START MY BUSINESS:**
Wanted to open a store with a personal unique vision that brings something different -- a local store with an international appeal, that incorpoartes a love of nature and modernity.

**ADVICE I WOULD GIVE TO WOMEN STARTING THEIR OWN BUSINESS:**
You're doing this because you have your unique vision – keep that vision at the core of everything you do. Trust your instincts and maintain your vision.

**MISTAKE THAT I HOPE NOT TO REPEAT:**
Being talked into buying things that weren't consistent with our vision of the store.

**WHAT I LIKE MOST ABOUT OWNING A BUSINESS:**
Having genuine interaction with new people on an everyday basis. The positive feedback from customers. Collaborating with local artists and creating original products.

**WHAT I LIKE LEAST ABOUT OWNING A BUSINESS:**
The risks involved: such as when the upstairs neighbors were tripping on LSD and overflowed their bathtub, which caused thousands of dollars in ceiling and merchandise damage.

**FAVORITE GUILTY PLEASURE SHOPPING PLACES:**
Behind the Post Office in the Upper Haight; Dema in the Mission; Dish and Flight OO1 in Hayes Valley; Mingle in Cow Hollow; Dress in the Marina; Wishbone in the Inner Sunset; AB Fits downtown; Delilah Crown in North Beach; Erika Tanov in Upper Fillmore

## 13. Mercury Fitness High Performance Pilates Center

2904 Laguna St.  415-567-9009 (fitness)
www.mercuryfitness.com - Owner: Lara Hudson
Bestselling fitness video star Lara Hudson leads
a team of expert trainers with an aggressive approach to Pilates at her 2,100-square-foot spa-like
facility. Transform your physique at this candlelit,
high-design environment where vanity rules.
Special introductory and combination packages
are available at discounted rates for private, group
machine, and multi-level mat classes.

## 14. Neda's Flowers & Gifts

681 Haight St.  415-552-2920 (flowers)
Owner: Yvonne Lam
Neda's Flowers & Gifts is a soothing space full of
carefully handled flowers and unusual gifts made
from natural materials. Vases of wood, bamboo,
and stone are for sale, along with handmade
soaps scented with plant essences. Jewel-like
miniature nature photos, candles, chocolates,
honey, and organic compost fill the shop. Neda's
provides full FTD/TeleFlora service and prompt
local delivery.

## 15. Queen of the Meadow

51 Divisadero St.  415-355-1051 (boutique)
Owner: Susan Jones
San Francisco trendsetters flock to this cutting-
edge boutique (located off the beaten path) because they know they'll discover something new
and unique. Current favorites are Sass & Bide
and Mike & Chris. The shop handpicks garments
from trendy designers, and showcases emerging
and local designers. All this is combined with
customer service in a cozy atmosphere.

## 16. Shoe Biz

1420 Haight St.  415.861.0313  (shoes)
www.shoebizsf.com - Owner: Nooshin Ansarinia
In business since 1979, Shoe Biz has grown and
now features four stores on Haight. The shops sell
hard-to-find and alternative styles, but each has a
specialty, from rare sneakers from Puma and Onit-
suka Tiger, to high-end shoes from Europe, to an
adidas concept shop. Check out the other locations
at 1422, 1446, and 1553 Haight.

## 17. Stuf
1612 Haight St. 415-551-STUF (boutique)
Manager: Janna Cruz
Accessories galore at this unobtrusive "little" shop, including a few exclusive designs from local artists. You'll find handbags, clutches, wallets, jewelry, watches, hats, and more. From the eye-catching and structured to the vibrant and funky – it's all at Stuf

## 18. True
1427 Haight St. 415-626-2331 (boutique)
www.trueclothing.net
Women's Buyer: Janelle Sinclair
True's women's store is overflowing with flavor. In the upbeat boutique, find everything from a special tee to a pair of premium jeans. True's roots are in urban clothing, but you can also discover unique streetwear brands and young contemporary lines to satisfy all your tastes.

## 19. Villains, Villains Vault, Villains Shoes
1672 Haight St./1653 Haight St. 415-626-5939 (boutique)
www.villainssf.com - Manager: Suzy Waters
Welcome to the largest selection of denim in San Francisco. The shop specializes in unique, hard-to-find items for any budget. Throw in our amazingly diverse shoe styles and you truly have a one-stop shopping experience. Well-trained staff makes sure you leave looking like a million bucks.

## 20. Wasteland
1660 Haight St. 415-863-3150 (boutique)
www.thewasteland.com - Owner: Cheryl Cohen
Wasteland is the destination for the finest in vintage, designer, and modern clothing. They offer a dazzling selection of apparel and accessories that have been the inspiration for many stylists, designers, and celebrities. Voted the "best place to sell your clothes" in Rolling Stone magazine, Wasteland is the place to shop and be seen.

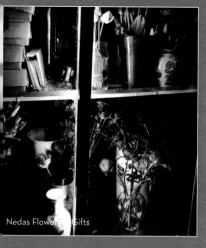

Nedas Flowers & Gifts

Queen of the Meadow

Stuf

Villians

Wasteland

Earthsong

## Manda Heron

BODY TIME

1465 Haight St.
415-551-1070  www.bodytime.com

*"It is possible to be socially conscious and still pamper and take care of your body!"*

### INSPIRATION/MOTIVATION FOR STARTING MY BUSINESS:

My mother and aunt opened the original store, which at that time was called "The Body Shop" in 1970, on Telegraph Avenue in Berkeley. They were inspired by the French perfumeries and wanted to create a fun and unique twist on that theme. They were in their 50's and their children were grown so they had a lot of creative juices with which to launch their business.

### MY ROLE MODELS/MENTORS:

Since I worked with my mother and aunt, they were my mentors in the beginning. Over the years I have begun to align myself with other local, small businesses with the goal of providing a great product as well as maintaining a socially conscious business.

### ADVICE I WOULD GIVE TO WOMEN STARTING THEIR OWN BUSINESS?

Think small, go slow, stay true to your original vision and don't try to over expand Essentially, don't get greedy.

### MISTAKE THAT I HOPE NOT TO REPEAT

Opening too many stores too quickly.

### WHAT I LIKE MOST ABOUT OWNING A BUSINESS:

Providing employment is important to me. Quite a few folks here have been with Bod Time since the beginning and many others for years.  This business is really made up of the people who work it.  I also enjoy the products we produce immensely; I use them daily and believe in them so I feel good about selling them.

### WHAT I LIKE LEAST ABOUT OWNING A BUSINESS:

It becomes difficult to reinvent your business, to keep it fresh.  Our customers, employees and I all want things to be new yet have a feeling of consistency and that a challenge.

## 21. The Yoga Loft

321 Divisadero St.  415-626-5638 (yoga)
www.theloftsf.com
Owners: Jane Dobson & Meg Whitbread
In offering daily yoga with teachers from a variety of traditions, The Yoga Loft honors the roots and origins of the practice, creating a meaningful framework for doing the practice today. The studio offers a full schedule of yoga classes, back care series, martial arts classes, lectures, workshops, and a comprehensive, ongoing educational program to explore the depth and breadth of yoga.

Notes:

# HAYES VALLEY/CIVIC CENTER

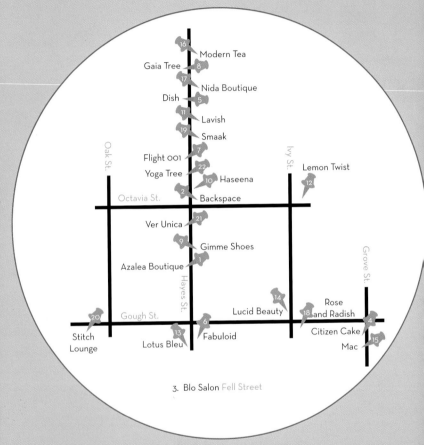

16 Modern Tea
Gaia Tree 8
17
Nida Boutique
Dish 5
11 Lavish
19 Smaak
Flight 001 7
22
Yoga Tree 10 Haseena
2
Octavia St. Backspace
21
Ver Unica
9 Gimme Shoes
1
Azalea Boutique

Oak St.

Ivy St.
Lemon Twist
12

Hayes St.

Grove St.

Lucid Beauty 14
Rose
18 and Radish
Gough St. 4
6 Citizen Cake
20 Fabuloid 15
Stitch 13 Mac
Lounge Lotus Bleu

3. Blo Salon Fell Street

Symphony & Opera aficionados frequent the many eclectic restaurants and bars in the area, but savvy shoppers in the know snap up bargains & couture-worthy finds from some of the most up-and-coming designers in town.

### 1. Azalea Boutique & Z Beauty Lounge

411 Hayes St.  415-861-9888 (boutique)

www.azaleasf.com

Owners: Catherine Chow & Corina Nurimba

Azalea is an eclectic lifestyle emporium that meshes niche clothing and accessory lines with an escapist nail bar called Z Beauty Lounge, a haute hideout in the back of the boutique. They are fashion and lifestyle connoisseurs who lovingly transform their luxe cherry-hued space into a de-facto lounge for cocktail parties.

### 2. Backspace

508 Hayes St.  415-701-7112 (boutique)

Owner: Susan Jones

This trendsetting boutique is a fashion-forward destination for locals and visitors alike. Backspace impressive mixture of must-have lines, along with up-and-coming and local designers, have made it a favorite with stylists and fashion editors. Current favorites are Grey Ant and Imitation of Christ denim. This ultra hip shop is the place to find unusual pieces you won't find in other boutiques.

### 3. Blo Salon

500 Fell St.  415-987-7092 (pamper)

www.beheadedsalon.com

Manager/Stylist: Chris Broom

Blo Salon in hip Hayes Valley has a casual vibe—think classic vintage meets industrial modern—which perfectly matches the flavor of the many boutiques and restaurants in the neighborhood. Chris, Robin, and Hilary offer experienced, personalized haircutting and coloring services in a fun atmosphere. The salon features Davines and PureOlogy products; wedding parties are a specialty.

### 4. Citizen Cake

399 Grove St.  415-861-2228 (eats)

www.citizencake.com

Executive Chef/Owner: Elizabeth Falkner

Citizen Cake is San Francisco's favorite dessert destination and trend-setting restaurant and bar. For dinner, try the sous-vide chicken cacciatore or ribeye with horseradish ice cream, but don't leave without a postmodern dessert. The Carrot Keiki is a parfait of re-thought carrot cake, while Something Chocolate This Way Comes is a sexy chocolate concoction.

## Desiree Alexander

DISH

541 Hayes St.
415-252-5997

*"Try to have a thick skin — the business world is not an easy place. Also, always try to grow and change with your business, otherwise you will get stuck in a rut."*

### INSPIRATION/MOTIVATION FOR STARTING MY BUSINESS:

My mom and dad had their own business and I watched them be dedicated to their vision for the business and the family. I guess I never considered not owning my own business, it's in our blood.

### HOW MUCH MONEY DID IT TAKE TO START?

I started the business with 50,000, but that was 10 years ago.

### MY ROLE MODELS/MENTORS:

My mom is my biggest inspiration. She has an enormous creative talent. And she has always been a fashion icon of mine. I also worked for a few female small business owners that really inspired me...Erica Tanov, the designer, is one of them.

### WHAT I LIKE MOST ABOUT OWNING A BUSINESS:

I love my clients and my employees. I feel very proud of my business but it wouldn't be anything with out good employees.

### WHAT I LIKE LEAST ABOUT OWNING A BUSINESS:

Being on call 24/7... You always bring the stress home.

### PEOPLE WOULD BE SURPRISED THAT I...

I do not have a huge closet full of clothes. I have learned to be very selective and only buy things that I love... I try to encourage my clients to do the same. It's the Dish motto.

### PERSONAL TIME OFF INDULGENCE:

Spending time with my son, playing in the backyard on a sunny day, and date night with my husband.

### FAVORITE GUILTY PLEASURE SHOPPING PLACE:

New York City. I have been buying a lot of home stuff. I love John Derian and ABC Carpet.

## HOW MUCH MONEY DID IT TAKE TO START?

We did all the design and build out work, so it only cost us $60,000.

## ADVICE WE WOULD GIVE TO WOMEN STARTING THEIR OWN BUSINESS:

Be confident of your decisions. There will always be people who will make you doubt your choices. Be passionate, work hard and have fun!

## MISTAKE WE HOPE NOT TO REPEAT:

Hiring the wrong employees. Your employees will make or break your business. Find a team that will help you grow your passion!

## WHAT WE LIKE MOST ABOUT OWNING A BUSINESS:

The customer and employee relationships you build. There is nothing more rewarding than happy customers and employees.

## WHAT WE LIKE LEAST ABOUT OWNING A BUSINESS:

The hours. You love it so much that you're constantly working!

## PEOPLE WOULD BE SURPRISED THAT...

Corina and I are closer than ever. Our partnership has grown into a lasting friendship.

## FAVORITE GUILTY PLEASURE SHOPPING PLACE:

Mango and H&M

## PERSONAL TIME OFF INDULGENCE:

Sleep

# Catherine Chow & Corina Nurimba

### AZALEA BOUTIQUE AND Z BEAUTY LOUNGE

411 Hayes St.
415-861-9888
www.azaleasf.com

*"Our inspiration came from our passion for clothes! Through the success of our private trunk shows, it inspired us to open a place where people can find unique clothing."*

## 5. Dish

541 Hayes St.  415-252-5997 (boutique)
Owner: Desiree Alexander
Dish is one of those stores that has a cult
following, and it's easy to see why after
meeting owner and retail veteran Desiree
Alexander. She's put together a great collection
of sophisticated yet edgy and modern clothing.
You can find fresh contemporary lines such
as Twelth Street by Cynthia Vincent, Rebecca
Taylor, and Development. The jewelry selection
is just as amazing.

## 6. Fabuloid

336 Hayes St.  415-355-0400 (boutique)
www.fabuloid.com - Manager: Silkie McKee
This shop invests in the city's artisans, locally producing ladies' and men's apparel to
old-school quality standards. Besides being
meticulously made, garments are astonishingly
affordable, because they are made from ends-
of-runs of extravagant materials the store buys
at great prices. You're buying direct from the
artists, with no shipping, packaging, or retailer
markup. What's not to like about that?

## 7. Flight 001

525 Hayes St.  415-487-1001 (boutique)
www.flight001.com
Director of Stores: Rachel O'Marra
Inspired by the high-style airline travel of the
1950s, this one-stop travel shop will redefine
your style on the go. Flight 001 recreates the
thrill of an international airport with merchandise
that addresses every travel need with style and
comfort. Flight 001 offers consumers a brilliantly
edited selection of cosmetics, carry-on bags,
guidebooks, electronics, and travel accessories.

## 8. Gaia Tree

575 Hayes St.  415-255-4848 (pamper)
www.gaiatree.com - Owner: Holly Zoffoli
A haven for locals and savvy visitors who crave
delicious yet healthy spa treats, this apothecary
is located in a quaint Victorian. Services are
offered in a peaceful, friendly environment, and
you may choose locally handcrafted balms or
the best lotions from Greece, Germany, and
Japan. Sundari, Epicuren, and In Fiore are some
of the favorites you'll find here.

### 9. Gimme Shoes

416 Hayes St.   415-864-0691 (shoes)
www.gimmeshoes.com - Co-owner: Leigh Stackpole
After 20-plus years, Gimme Shoes still offers amazing footwear and accessories. The store has evolved from a tiny hip outpost in the Tenderloin, offering up-to-the-minute London street styles, to three locations in the city, frequented by an international clientele with excellent taste.

### 10. Haseena

526 Hayes St.   415-252-1104 (boutique)
Owner: Rajinder Sweeney
Haseena stands for beauty. Nestled in the heart of Hayes Valley, this boutique offers stylish, chic clothing for men and women who want to feel beautiful (or handsome) for every occasion. The shop promotes local designers—Mary Green Lingerie, Western Wear, and Tokyo Bay Watches, among others. Come see the main attraction, Pemba, the owner's handsome German shepherd.

### 11. lavish

540 Hayes St.   415-565-0540 (décor)
www.shoplavish.com - Owner: Elizabeth Leu
What, exactly, is lavish? 'la-vish; 1. the perfect place to pamper yourself or someone you love with a delicious display of home accessories, kid's clothing and toys, women's apparel, and luxurious bath and beauty products; 2. a sunny little boutique in Hayes Valley dedicated to distinctive merchandise featuring local and independent designers; 3. your one-stop shop for baby showers, birthdays, or browsing.

### 12. Lemon Twist

537 Octavia Blvd.  415-558-9699 (boutique)
www.lemontwist.net - Owner: Danette Scheib
For modern clothing with a twist, visit this spirited Hayes Valley boutique. Six-year design veteran Danette Scheib and her husband Eric continue to prove themselves each season with their collection of clothing and tees. This clean, airy space combines a boutique and design studio, so if you like a piece but would prefer a different fabric, they'll customize one for you.

Azalea

Backspace

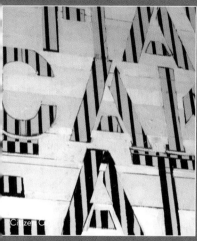

Citizen Clothing

Fabuloid

Flight 001

Gimme Shoes

## INSPIRATION/MOTIVATION FOR STARTING MY BUSINESS

In addition to my travels, I was also inspired to start the business by my art history background. I went to graduate school in art history at Stanford (received M.A. and Ph.D. candidacy), and worked in several museums, included the Cantors Arts Center at Stanford and The Metropolitan Museum of Art in New York.

## MY ROLE MODELS/MENTORS:

I appreciate the work of designers like Sherri Donghia of Donghia who updates and modernizes Asian textile traditions, and Liz Galbraith and Ephraim Paul of Galbraith and Paul who update and revive hand block printing techniques in a workshop environment.

## ADVICE I WOULD GIVE TO WOMEN STARTING THEIR OWN BUSINESS:

Talk to people in the business before starting, don't be afraid to think out of the box, research your products well and make sure you're bringing something new to the scene, and constantly expose yourself to new designs and environments.

## WHAT I LIKE MOST ABOUT OWNING A BUSINESS:

I like the flexibility and creative potential. I mix my time between working on residential design projects and developing sources for my retail shop. I'm always learning and experiencing new challenges.

## WHAT I LIKE LEAST ABOUT OWNING A BUSINESS:

I don't have "fixed" hours and end up working a lot. There's always something new to do or pursue. Since my vendors are in France and Southeast Asia, it's sometimes harder to communicate and make sure they understand my design requirements and concerns.

## Jeannie Fraise

### LOTUS BLEU

327 Hayes St.
415-861-2700
www.lotusbleudesign.com

"I started my interior design business in 2003 and opened the store this year. I was inspired to start my business after traveling extensively around the world with my husband during the past 15 years. He is French and his family is from Madagascar in Africa. We travel regularly to France and Southeast Asia, exploring new sources for art and home decor."

### 13. Lotus Bleu
327 Hayes St. 415-861-2700 (décor)
www.lotusbleudesign.com - Owner: Jeannie Fraise

Interior designer Jeannie Fraise travels to France
and Southeast Asia to bring her customers a
unique selection of home textiles, furniture, lighting, and art. With vibrant colors, bold patterns,
and luxurious fabrics, her products offer a modern
twist on traditional materials and motifs. At her
cozy store, Jeannie can help you design linens,
reupholster furniture, or develop a larger decorating project.

### 14. Lucid Beauty
313 Ivy St. 415-252-9591 (pamper)
www.lucidbeauty.com - Owner: Cheryl Lucid

This quiet, private Hayes Valley skincare boutique
specializes in customized skin care treatments,
threading hair removal, brow shaping, and cor-
rective skin peels. It also features product lines
from Cosmedix, Enessa, Blodroga, Epicener, and
True Mineral Cosmetics, and soy-based candles
by Pure White.

### 15. MAC
387 Grove St. 415-863-3011 (boutique)
Owner: Chris Ospital

Located in free-wheeling Hayes Valley, MAC
(Modern Appealing Clothing) specializes in
emerging designers from Europe, Asia, and San
Francisco with a broad stroke of Belgian designers. The new Lanvin collection offers "haberdashery with a twist" for the man in your life;
A.F. Vandevorst's seamed hosiery and lingerie
are a very sexy gift for your femme fatale (or
inner vixen).

### 16. Modern Tea
602 Hayes St. 415-626-5406 (tea)
www.moderntea.com - Owner: Alice Cravens

Modern Tea is a restaurant, tea salon, and retail
destination serving lunch through dinner, weekend brunch, and of course, tea. A sunlit room
welcomes you, the menu features local, organic
fare, and retail items that support earth-friendly
business make for an enjoyable respite whenever you find yourself near the Civic Center.

### 17. Nida Boutique

544 Hayes St.  415-552-4670 (boutique)
Managers: Jamie Hillman & Lauren Benson
This European-owned boutique stocks clothing
and accessories for men and women.  Inside you
will find friendly service, good music, and beautiful
clothing.  For men, choose from designers such as
Neil Barrett, Juan & Carlos, Masons, and Junya
Watanabe.  For women, we carry the hard-to-find
Isabel Marant, Paul & Joe, Marc by Marc Jacobs,
Emilio Pucci, and Vanessa Bruno.

### 18. Rose and Radish

460 Gough St.  415-864-4988 (flowers)
www.roseandradish.com - Owner: Cate Kellison
This atelier has been transformed into a gallery
that will showcase pieces around a theme.
Kellison and her talented staff have composed
displays of design objects—some to adorn your
tabletop, some to light your way, and some simply because you won't want to live without them.
The gallery will continue to take special orders,
and flowers will always be showcased.

### 19. Smaak

528 Hayes St.  415-503-1430 (boutique)
Owner: Susannah Gaterud
Looking for Scandinavian fashions? Smaak—
Dutch for "taste"—has your answer, carrying
women's and men's clothes primarily from
Sweden, Denmark and Finland. From simple to
elegant, Smaak's designs consist of everything
from the basic tee to the collared shirt, all
marked by a sleek, fashion-forward aesthetic.

### 20. Stitch Lounge

182 Gough St.  415-431-3739 (sewing)
www.stitchlounge.com - Owners: Melissa Alvarado,
Hope Meng & Melissa Rannels
Stitch is an urban sewing lounge that provides an
inspirational environment for people to express
their individuality by creating their own fashion.
Tools, resources, and advice are provided in a comfortable, professional workspace. Picture a modern
sewing circle, where you can take group or private
classes, rent time on sewing machines, or browse
through racks filled with clothing by local designers.

Lotus Bleu

MAC

Nida Boutique

Rose & Radish

Smaack

Stitch Lounge

## INSPIRATION/MOTIVATION FOR START-ING MY BUSINESS:

I've been in the fitness business since 1985. My yoga practice made such a difference in my life – it helped to calm my mind, heal old injuries and I naturally turned my personal training clients into private yoga clients.

## MY ROLE MODEL/MENTOR:

My husband, Tim Dale for the business – he makes things happen! I wouldn't have made the leap – he's a leaper! If he says something he does it.

## ADVICE I WOULD GIVE TO WOMEN STARTING THEIR OWN BUSINESS:

Choose something you have a serious pas-sion for – don't open a dog food store if you don't like dogs! When you jump in, swim! No one is going to do it for you.

## MISTAKE THAT I HOPE NOT TO REPEAT:

Not ironing out every single detail, no mat-ter how small, before gong forward. And not getting everything in writing.

## WHAT I LIKE MOST ABOUT OWNING A BUSINESS:

People get to do yoga! It's life changing! I feel we are positively making a change in so many people's life – we get to provide a space for teachers to do what they love to do – being able to help people on a larger scale than just ourselves.

## WHAT I LIKE LEAST ABOUT OWNING A BUSINESS:

I got so busy with the business side that I no longer had time to teach – which is what I love to do.

## FAVORITE GUILTY PLEASURE SHOP-PING PLACE:

Saks Fifth Ave!

## PERSONAL TIME OFF INDULGENCE:

Eating good food and drinking good wine with my husband.

## Tara Dale

YOGA TREE

519 Hayes St.
415-626-9707
www.yogatreesf.com

*"I chose to feature different styles of yoga, because just as there are many rivers to the ocean – there are many different styles of yoga... I don't believe there is just one way to do things."*

## 21. Ver Unica

437B Hayes St.  415-431-0688 (boutique)
www.ver-unica.com
Co-owners: Cindy Spade & Willow O'Brien
This vintage boutique dresses fashionistas who
appreciate a mixture of fine clothing and accessories from any era, along with indie designer
creations that leave you wanting more. Don't
miss out! Get on the shop's mailing list to stay in
the know about trunk shows, art openings, and
sales. Ver Unica knows how to do it up right.

## 22. Yoga Tree

519 Hayes St.  415-626-9707 (yoga)
www.yogatreesf.com  - Owner: Tara Dale
With four studios, Yoga Tree brings you the best
instructors the Bay Area has to offer. In studios
that are clean, warm, and supportive, they offer
a variety of styles of yoga and all of the classes
share one thing in common: a comfortable and
safe space in which to explore the body, mind,
and soul.

Notes:

# Cow Hollow

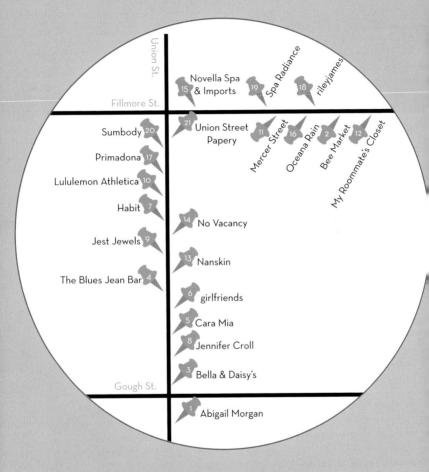

Union St.

Fillmore St.

Novella Spa & Imports 15
Spa Radiance 19
rileyjames 18

Sumbody 20
Primadona 17
Lululemon Athletica 10
Habit 7
Jest Jewels 9
The Blues Jean Bar 4

21 Union Street Papery
Mercer Street 11
Oceana Rain 16
Bee Market 2
My Roommate's Closet 12

14 No Vacancy
13 Nanskin
6 girlfriends
5 Cara Mia
8 Jennifer Croll
3 Bella & Daisy's

Gough St.

1 Abigail Morgan

1. Abigail Morgan  2. Bee Market
3. Bella and Daisy's  4. The Blues Jean Bar
5. Cara Mia  6. girlfriends  7. Habit  8. Jennifer Croll  9. Jest Jewels
10. lululemon athletica  11. Mercer Street Salon  12. My Roommate's Closet
13. Nanskin  14. No Vacancy  15. Novella Spa & Imports  16. Oceana Rain
17. Primadona  Premier Skincare & Spa  18. riley james  19. Spa Radiance
20. sumbody  21. Union Street Papery

*Fun in the sun is a way of life for the fit and frisky 20 and 30-somethings who love their single status and their Starbucks. Hit Union Street for a cup of joe and a trendy outfit for that roof-top BBQ, then retire to one of the many sidewalk cafes for a Sunday afternoon cocktail.*

### 1. Abigail Morgan

1640 Union Street  415-567-1779 (boutique)
www.abigailmorgan.com - Co-owner: Abigail Piron
This boutique will make you feel right at home.
The comfortable, shabby chic décor is stocked
with your favorite collections from, Splendid,
Citizens of Humanity, Trina Turk, Milly, and Joie
(to name a few). You'll feel like you are going
through your dream closet. Make sure to check
out the spacious fitting rooms, constructed of old
vintage doors.

### 2. Bee Market

3030 Fillmore St.  415-292-2910 (décor)
www.bee-market.com - Owner: Virginie Wallace
Fusing classic and modern, the Bee Market collection is as functional as it is chic, sophisticated, and
beautiful. Create a customized piece or person-
alize a collection for your home or office. Each
customized piece is available in the highest-quality
hardwoods and premium fabrics, leathers, and
suedes. Bee Market creates timeless pieces with
modern elegance.

### 3. Bella and Daisy's

1750 Union St.  415-440-7007 (pets)
www.bellaanddaisys.com - Owner: Melissa Marshall
From "yappy" hour to dog birthday parties, this
San Francisco original is not to be missed. Find
everything from Juicy Couture clothing and
accessories to every style bed you can imagine.
Don't miss the bakery case with doggy cupcakes
and organic treats. Whether you think one collar
is plenty or you want your dog to dress like you,
you'll find it here.

### 4. The Blues Jean Bar

1827 Union St.  415-346-4280 (boutique)
www.thebluesjeanbar.com - Owner: Lady Reiss
Shopping for jeans is never an easy task, but the
staff at the Blues Jean Bar will help you find the
perfect pair to flatter your figure and fit your style.
Belly up to the bar for more than 35 brands of men
and women jeans. Just tell the "jeantender" your
waist size and the friendly staff will fit you.

## Donna O'Leary

AMBIANCE

1864 & 1858 Union Street
415.923.9797 & 415.923.9796
www.ambiancesf.com

"I love every aspect of fashion and helping women look more beautiful."

**HOW MUCH MONEY DID IT TAKE TO START?**
Roughly $200,000.

**MY ROLE MODELS/MENTORS:**
My mother was a stylish, smart woman who taught me to sew when I was five years old. She ran her own successful business. I miss her every day.

**ADVICE THAT I WOULD GIVE TO WOMEN STARTING THEIR OWN BUSINESS:**
Learn from someone who already knows how to do it. Apprentice yourself in a similar successful business. Be humble, know that you do not know everything and be prepared to learn. Also, it is often easier to purchase an existing business rather than start a new one. You can change it after you buy it.

**MISTAKE THAT I HOPE NOT TO REPEAT:**
Pulling an all-nighter that did not turn out to be necessary.

**WHAT I LIKE MOST ABOUT OWNING A BUSINESS:**
The creativity and freedom to do it your way. Seeing your ideas come to life and actually work. Working with other talented people (my employees). Letting them be creative and add to the business' success.

**WHAT I LIKE LEAST ABOUT OWNING A BUSINESS:**
You are always on – Ambiance runs 7 days a week. Bottom line, the buck stops with you.

**PEOPLE WOULD BE SURPRISED THAT I...**
Am 51 years old and do not fit in my own merchandise.

**FAVORITE GUILTY PLEASURE SHOPPING:**
Neiman Marcus' shoe salon in San Francisco; Bergdorf Goodman's shoe salon in NYC.

## Leslie Drapkin & Eleanor Carpenter

JEST JEWELS

1869 Union Street
415-563-8839 www.jestjewels.com

"Both Eleanor and I travel the world regularly for the treasure hunt that is our business, and though we just celebrated twenty years, it feels new and different constantly."

**INSPIRATION/MOTIVATION FOR START-ING OUR BUSINESS:**

To get out of the corporate world and develop our own corner of independence

**WHAT WE LIKE MOST ABOUT OWNING OUR OWN BUSINESS:**

Our customers and our community. Without them, we are nothing, so I love being very involved and love developing constant great customer service. I also love the endless discovery of new designers and fresh takes on old ideas. The 'hunt' is the thing.

**WHAT I LOVE ABOUT DOING BUSINESS IN SAN FRANCISCO:**

Everything. It is a beautiful, romantic city that is small enough for intimacy, and large enough for big ideas. Customers are loyal here and love to shop, which makes owning a business here wonderful, and the natural beauty of the city makes working in it a pleasure.

**FAVORITE GUILTY PLEASURE SHOP-PING PLACES:**

I love Jeremy's on 2nd St. for interesting or price designer clothes, Nest on Fillmore for old and new gift items and other things, La Rosa for vintage on Haight, and Workshop on Union St. for clothing and shoes.

**PERSONAL TIME OFF INDULGENCE:**

I love to play with my dogs and friends, scour the city for new restaurants and stores, frequent independent bookstores, and if I still have time I love to indulge in some of the great day spas that have popped up all over the city.

**ADVICE I WOULD GIVE TO WOMEN STARTING THEIR OWN BUSINESS:**

Love what you do...eat, breathe and sleep it until you work out your dream. Take risks but make them educated risks, have a business plan and sound goals, work hard, and don't forget to have fun!

## 5. Cara Mia

1814 Union Street  415-922-2272 (boutique)
www.caramiastores.com
You'll find some of the city's finest fashions and cutting edge designs in women's clothing, accessories, shoes, bags and jewelry at Cara Mia. If you see it in your favorite magazine - you might very well find it here. This boutique's claim to fame is their large stock of Jack Rogers sandals – the favorite shoe of none other than Jackie Kennedy.

## 6. girlfriends

1824 Union St.  415-673-9544 (boutique)
www.girlfriendsboutique.com
Co-owners: Katherine Ryan & Susan Margolis
This sweet boutique is as cozy as it sounds. Bring your closest friends along, throw yourselves on the sofa, and shop racks filled with Michael Stars tees, G-1 Basic Goods, Petit Bateau, along with dozens of other hip designers. Don't forget to pick up one of the store's signature logo items on your way out. The girlfriends fitted tee is a must have.

## 7. Habit

1905 Union St., Suite 1  415-441-3332 (pamper)
www.waxhabit.com - Owner: Carrie Maxwell
Habit is San Francisco's only waxing-specific boutique. Custom-blended care (pre- and post-service) and an avant-garde atmosphere provide a unique esthetic experience for regulars and visitors alike. Expert proprietress Maxwell will harm even the most squeamish first-timer (and a complimentary glass of wine never hurt anyone).

## 8. Jennifer Croll

1810 Union St.  415-749-1810 (boutique)
www.jennifercroll.com - Owner: Jennifer Croll
Jennifer Croll is a high-end men's and women's boutique featuring clothing by hot designers of the moment and classic designers with timeless styles. Find everything from casual wear to dressy evening wear and even bridal gowns. Listen to great music, catch a game on the plasma, or shoot a game of pool while shopping for the hippest clothes around.

### 9. Jest Jewels

1869 Union St.   415-563-8839 (jewelry)
www.jestjewels.com
Co-owners: Eleanor Carpenter & Leslie Drapkin
Get ready for a floor-to-ceiling feast for the senses: jewelry (both fine and fashion), handbags, hats, gift items, lingerie, and always a bit of the unexpected. And, if you don't see what you want, the owners will knock themselves out trying to get it for you. It is a trendy, upbeat hotspot and fun for both the customers and the owners.

### 10. lululemon athletica

1981 Union St.   415-776-5858 (boutique)
www.lululemon.com - Manager: Estee Fletter
Yoga-inspired athletic apparel company lululemon athletica was founded by a group of visionary athletes, in response to the exponential increase of female participation in sports and the belief that yoga is the way to maintain athletic excellence. The staff aspires to provide components to help customers achieve their athletic goals, to lead balanced, positive lives, and to feel amazing.

### 11. Mercer Street Salon

3012 Fillmore St.   415-674-4444 (pamper)
www.mercerstreetsalon.com
Owners: Jennifer Jordan, and Alicia Berberich
Finding the perfect salon? Not easy. Finding the perfect hairdresser? Next to impossible. Lucky for you, you've just discovered Mercer Street. Step into this ultra-modern salon and get ready to look your best. This place is all about the client – so you'll immediately notice less attitude and more service – not to mention complimentary cappuccinos and cupcakes.

### 12. My Roommate's Closet

3044 Fillmore St.   415-447-7703 (boutique)
www.myroommatescloset.com
Owners: Cate Corfman & Suzanne Lynch
My Roommate's Closet takes stock from fashion-forward boutiques in San Francisco, New York, and Los Angeles, and offers it at 50 percent off the original price. Bargain lovers in search of designer merchandise will leave looking chic, with the bonus of a few extra bucks in their bag. There are new arrivals all the time, so check back regularly.

Abigail Morgan

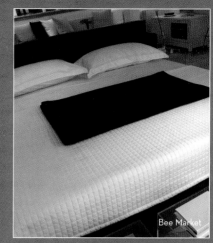

Bee Market

Bella & Daisy's

Girlfriend

Habit

Jennifer Croll

## INSPIRATION/MOTIVATION FOR STARTING MY BUSINESS:

The lack of unique shopping experiences in the city. When my roommate Cindy and I moved here from Austin, we could not find any of the designers we liked at any of the boutiques. Every store we went in was a carbon copy of the last.

## ADVICE I WOULD GIVE TO WOMEN STARTING THEIR OWN BUSINESS:

Hire a bookkeeper. It doesn't matter if it's an extra cost, it's well worth it. Also, never be embarrassed to ask questions. Nobody knows all the answers, not even you. It's really hard for women to stand up and say "I need help" – I think we want to prove ourselves so much, that we forget that asking questions is part of the learning process.

## MISTAKE THAT I HOPE NOT TO REPEAT:

I hate to say it, but automatically trusting what people say. You should ALWAYS get a second, and even a third, opinion. It sounds harsh, but no one looks out for your business the way you will... EVER.

## WHAT I LIKE MOST ABOUT OWNING A BUSINESS:

The joy and happiness that I get from doing what I love. No matter how hard things get, when a customer tells me how much they love the store, the clothes, the staff, it makes it all worth it. When you have an idea, and people are positively affected by it, the feeling is amazing.

## WHAT I LIKE LEAST ABOUT OWNING A BUSINESS:

In my industry, there is a lot of backstabbing and gossip. It's the only thing that ever makes me want to give up, but I just keep reminding myself that if you cut those people out, life is pretty good. People will always try to bring you down, only you can let them.

# Nicki Osina

RILEY JAMES

3027 Fillmore St.
415-775-7956
www.rileyjames.com

*"We opened our doors in November of 2002. Our staff is extremely knowledgeable and friendly. We are also willing to do personal shopping for our customers, privately at the store, or we will bring a rack of items to their home."*

## 13. Nanskin

1850 Union St., Suite 7  415-563-4024 (pamper)
www.nanskin.com - Owner: Nan Webb
Fresh, sexy, glowing skin is what you'll be raving
about when Nan facials you up using a cherry
pomegranate peel, chocolate scrub, or an epider-
mal growth factor rolled on with a frozen beauty
globe! Pampering at Nanskin includes wine, jazz
tunes, and generous skincare samples with your
extractions. For more fun, try a facial for two.

## 14. No Vacancy

1878 Union St.  415-885-8020 (boutique)
www.novacancysf.com - Owner: Fallon Frazier
Uncover the latest looks from some of the hottest
designers out of Los Angeles and New York,
including Siwy Denim, Morphine Generation, and
Religion. The store is about a feminine look with
a rock and roll vibe, and has up-to-the-minute
celebrity favorites. This cool, hidden hangout is
discreetly tucked away from busy traffic of Union
Street.

## 15. Novella Spa & Imports

2238 Union St.  415-673-1929 (pamper)
www.novellaspaandimports.com
Owner: Cheryl Chakler
The Novella Experience is a journey in healing
decadence. The spa/boutique provides a sanctu-
ary to nourish the traveler within us all. Whether
it's enjoying world-class hair, skin, or body services, or perusing the finest in furniture and gifts,
you are bound to leave Novella anticipating your
next escape to this haven of rejuvenation.

## 16. Oceana Rain

3024 Fillmore St. 415-346-2797 (boutique)
www.oceanarain.com - Owner: Oceana Rain Stuart
This boutique will tempt every woman's inner diva.
You'll find it hard to resist denim from Habitual and
shoes from Twelfth Street by Cynthia Vincent, not
to mention clothes by Rebecca Taylor, Catharine
Malandrino, Sass & Bide, Ya Ya, Alice & Olivia, and
Paul & Joe. The jewelry case is full of creations to
complement any outfit.

### 17. Primadona Premier Skincare & Spa

2103 Union St. 415-775-3614 (pamper)
www.primadonaskincare.com
Co-owner: Gabriela Spaccia
Primadona is a boutique spa owned and operated by Gabriela and Enzo Spaccia. With a background in biology and genetics, Gabriela combines skincare technology with esthetics to provide proper protocols. Enzo spent nearly 20 years as a representative for the finest skincare lines, and has consulted with the world's best spas.

### 18. riley james

3027 Fillmore St. 415-775-7956 (boutique)
www.rileyjames.com - Owner: Nicki Osina
riley james is a fashion-forward mecca providing hard-to-find labels mixed in with an amazing selection of jewelry and accessories. This men's and women's store features a knowledgeable staff and fresh beats for the ultimate shopping soundtrack, and mini-bulldog Piper is usually keeping watch from the window. Add to this exclusive pieces and you can see that riley james is a true original.

### 19. Spa Radiance

3011 Fillmore St. 415-346-6281 (pamper)
www.sparadiance.com
Owner: Galina Rovner & Angelina Umansky
Named by *Allure* magazine as one of the beauty pros A-lister's adore, Spa Radiance is renowned for its highly trained estheticians and therapists, who provide the latest in innovative and healing spa treatments. Located steps from Union Street' fashionable boutiques, Spa Radiance is a chic, inviting hideaway for spa-goers who know the importance of life's luxuries.

### 20. sumbody

2167 Union St. 415-775-6343 (pamper)
www.sumbody.com - Owner: Deborah Burns
sumbody is a pure skincare line that prides itself on using all-natural, finest quality products. Each item is handmade to ensure the beneficial goodness of every scrumptious body treat, without chemicals or preservatives. At sumbody, you'll find such unique products as Dead Sea bath salts, organic sugar body scrubs, red currant lip balm, and delicious natural handmade soaps.

Jest Jewels

lululemon athletica

Mercer Street

riley james

Spa Radiance

**kaleidosoap**

All roads lead to Rome, or so they say. Although we're all on many different paths, our desired destinations are usually not that different. As we look at the magic of a kaleidoscope and see the many different but equally beautiful patterns it can create, it reminds us that there is no "right" way, as long as we're on the way. No matter how different the pieces or angle, it's always equally and uniquely beautiful. A new perspective and expanse of ourselves.

sumbody

## ADVICE THAT I WOULD GIVE TO WOMEN STARTING THEIR OWN BUSINESS:

Realize exactly what makes your business special and focus on making that stronger- you can't go wrong! And recognize that your customers are vital to your success.

## WHAT I LIKE MOST ABOUT OWNING A BUSINESS:

The freedom to create my own space, which includes everything from staffing to décor and product.

## WHAT I LIKE LEAST ABOUT OWNING A BUSINESS:

No matter what, its 24-7 even when you are off, you are on, when it's yours-this has way more upsides than downsides.

## PEOPLE WOULD BE SURPRISED THAT I..

Have been involved in the paper industry for 20 years. It was my first real job!

## Stacey Bush

UNION STREET PAPERY

2162 Union St.
415-563-0200
www.unionstreetpapery.com

## FAVORITE GUILTY PLEASURE SHOPPING PLACE:

Nest – incredible merchandising, always eclectic selection of house wares and gifts!

## PERSONAL TIME OFF INDULGENCE:

Vacationing in Mexico.

"I found a business I loved at an early age that led to my entrepreneurial spirit and kept me far from the corporate world."

## 21. Union Street Papery

2162 Union St.  415-563-0200  (gifts)
www.unionstreetpapery.com
Owner: Stacey Bush

Paper fanatics crave this unique boutique's infinite selection of chic invitations, stylish stationery, charming cards, and wonderful wrap and ribbon. Their specialty is putting your personality in print. The Papery's savvy staff custom creates everything from save-the-dates to wedding ensembles, baby announcements to birthday invites, social stationery to holiday cards.

Notes:

# MISSION/POTRERO

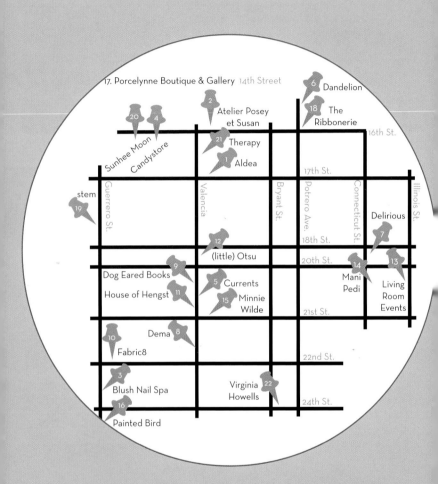

17. Porcelynne Boutique & Gallery  14th Street

6  Dandelion

2  Atelier Posey
et Susan

18  The
Ribbonerie

16th St.

20  4  Sunhee Moon
Candystore

21  Therapy

1  Aldea

17th St.

Guerrero St.

Valencia

Bryant St.

Potrero Ave.

Connecticut St.

Illinois St.

stem
19

Delirious
7

12

(little) Otsu

18th St.

20th St.

9  Dog Eared Books

14  Mani
Pedi

13  Living
Room
Events

House of Hengst  11

5  Currents

15  Minnie
Wilde

21st St.

10  Dema  8

Fabric8

22nd St.

3  Blush Nail Spa

22  Virginia
Howells

24th St.

16  Painted Bird

The dot.com boom gentrified this haven for thrift shops & used bookstores, while leaving the local Latino flavor intact. Check out some of
the hottest nightclubs in town while indulging in the area's plethora of
funky boutiques, soothing spas & decadent eateries.

### 1. Aldea
3338 17th St., Suite 100B  415-865-9807 (décor)
www.aldeahome.com - Owner: Johanna Bialkin
Wish your home could look as fabulous as your favorite store (or vice versa)? Have it all at Aldea from the comfy bed with the perfect silk coverlet to the hipster clothes in the closet. It's all for sale in this 1,500-square-foot interactive apartment. Peruse five stylized "rooms" filled with exotic home products from around the world.

### 2. Atelier Posey et Susan
2720 16th St.  415-776-6367 (décor)
www.jfc3.com/atelier.html
Owner: Posey and Susan Tibbon
Enjoy this Mission District studio with a clear conscience and an eye for the unique. Everything, from meticulously appliquéd and crocheted clothing and accessories to exquisite prints, is completely handmade by Posey and Susan. In the magic atelier, the sisters create fun carryalls and magnificent wedding gifts, recently featured at the Oakland Museum and Jewish Museum of San Francisco.

### 3. Blush Nail Spa
1003 Guerrero St.  415-285-6245 (pamper)
www.blushnailspa.com - Owner: Angie Duong
Blush Nail Spa offers a variety of spa services, and many are accompanied by aromatherapy. The spa offers many different hand and foot therapy treatments, including the popular Callus Buster Pedicure.

### 4. Candystore
3153 16th St.  415-863-8143 (boutique)
www.candystore-sf.com
Owners: Jennifer Jones & Jenny Klowden
Candystore fuses the realms of fashion, home, art, craft, and music. The boutique showcases the work of independent designers, artists, and design collectives from exotic locales. Add to that the hottest indie clothing labels and vintage finds, and you'll see that Candystore's hard-to-find design anything but ordinary.

## INSPIRATION/MOTIVATION FOR STARTING MY BUSINESS:

I loved the location and wanted to expand.

## HOW MUCH MONEY DID IT TAKE TO START?

A lot, make sure you have enough because you'll need more.

## MY ROLE MODEL/MENTOR:

My husband, with his great "go for it" attitude.

## PEOPLE WOULD BE SURPRISED THAT I...

Was a cook for 8 years.

## FAVORITE SHOPPING:

Any other small boutiques. I try to support small business owners as much as possible.

## PERSONAL TIME OFF INDULGENCE:

A great massage.

# Maxine Siu

STEM

3690 18th St.
415-861-7836
www.stemsf.com

*"Love what you do. Make sure you find a great location. Be patient and confident that it will work."*

## INSPIRATION/MOTIVATION FOR STARTING MY BUSINESS:

A wish that San Francisco had a medium-priced nail shop with fun things to buy that was a safe place where tools were sanitized between each and every client.

## MISTAKE THAT I HOPE NOT TO REPEAT:

Trusting that others are doing their jobs and not checking up on them.

## WHAT I LIKE MOST ABOUT OWNING A BUSINESS:

That my staff and I can make people's day when they come to our shop.

## WHAT I LIKE LEAST ABOUT OWNING A BUSINESS:

Managing the staff and the schedule.

## PEOPLE WOULD BE SURPRISED THAT I:

Was an Art Director in Advertising before opening this nail spa.

## FAVORITE GUILTY PLEASURE SHOPPING PLACE:

The lingerie department at Nordstrom.

## PERSONAL TIME OFF INDULGENCE:

Massages at Nob Hill Spa and facials at Le Sanctuaire.

# Kelly Hensley

MANI PEDI

1447 20th St.
415-401-MANI
www.manipedi.com

*"When you open, you realize quickly that you are not your own boss — every client that walks through your door is your boss."*

5. Currents

911 Valencia St.  415-648-2015  (pamper)
www.currentssf.com
Owners: Akira Kobayashi & Mari Uehilo
You'll know Currents is near when the scent of
green tea soap, roasted chestnut candles, and
homemade hibiscus bath salts drifts by. Step inside and indulge your senses. From animal slippers
to locally crafted lavender eye pillows and jewelry,
teapots, and sake sets, you'll find that special gift,
artfully (and complimentarily) wrapped and ready
to make someone happy.

6. Dandelion

55 Potrero Ave.  415-436-9500 (décor)
www.tampopo.com
Dandelion was established in 1968, offering
interesting gifts and décor for the home at
affordable prices. It eventually turned to direct
import for well-designed merchandise from all
over the world. Approximately 60 percent of
its current inventory is directly imported for
Dandelion.

7. Delirious

17 Connecticut St.  415-641-4086 (shoes)
www.getdelirious.com - Owner: Amy J. Boe
Find your new favorite pair of shoes every time
you stop in this jewel box of a shoe store in
Potrero Hill, whether it's a comfortable pair for
cruising around town, office-appropriate shoes
you actually look forward to wearing, or hot-mama
night-on-the-town heels. Delirious also carries
men's shoes and a fabulous selection of purses
and accessories.

8. Dema

1938 Valencia St.  415-206-0500 (boutique)
www.godemago.com - Owner: Dema Grim
Dema caters to independently minded, eclectic
women of all ages. In-house designer Dema Grim
doesn't follow trends but sorts through a hodge-
podge of influences to come up with her signature
twisted classics. Also available is a well-edited
selection of sweaters, tees, jewelry, hosiery, and
handbags.

### 9. Dog Eared Books
900 Valencia St.  415-282-1901 (books)
www.dogearedbooks.com
Owner: Kate Rosenberger
Reflecting the flavor of the Mission district in which it resides, Dog Eared is large and eclectic—you'll find anarchist magazines next to Vanity Fair, Nina Simone CDs next to Joy Division, and Michelle Tea poetry next to Chaucer. The shop pays cash and trades for your used books, and sells both new and used titles.

### 10. fabric8
3318 22nd St.  415-647-5888  (boutique)
www.fabric8.com - Owner: Olivia Ongpin
fabric8 has featured unique goods by urban independent designers for more than a decade. The company was founded by Olivia Ongpin and Antony Quintal, who perceived the Internet as th ideal medium to support creative design. fabric8 has grown to represent many aspects of indie fashion, music, art, and culture, and continues to promote do-it-yourself businesses, both online an in this boutique.

### 11. House of Hengst
924 Valencia St.  415-642-0841 (boutique)
www.houseofhengst.com - Owner: Susan Hengst
With bolts of fabric in the back and a small, hip collection, House of Hengst feels like something you'd stumble upon in New York City, not Valencia Street. In fact, owner/designer Susan Hengst splits her time between San Francisco and her West Village studio, in order to create a well-priced mix of whimsical jumpsuits, sassy bloomers, and expertly tailored pants.

### 12. Little Otsu
849 Valencia St.  415-255-7900 (boutique)
www.littleotsu.com  - Owner: Yvonne Chen
Find a creative selection of inspired, handmade, and fairly made paper goods, tees, and accessories from around the country in this Mission neighborhood shop. Store exclusives include a li of limited-edition, sweatshop-free artist tees. Th shop also serves as headquarters for Little Otsu publishing, whose line of paper products is featu throughout the store.

Wildea

Currents

Dema

Dog Eared Books

Minnie Wilde

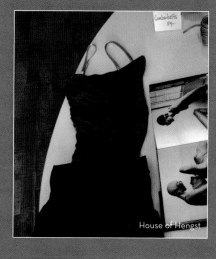
House of Hengst

**INSPIRATION/MOTIVATION FOR START-ING MY BUSINESS:**

The immediate gratification of a retail out-let. I enjoy interacting with my customers.

**HOW MUCH MONEY DID IT TAKE TO START?**

Not much, $7,000-10,000.

**MY ROLE MODELS/MENTORS:**

Terri Horlamus of Seattle's New York Fashion Academy taught me the basics of clothing design. Ben and Chris Ospital who co-own M.A.C. in San Francisco have encouraged and inspired me tremendously in the past 15 years.

**WHAT I LIKE MOST ABOUT OWNING A BUSINESS:**

Being in control. I've been self-employed for 20 years. I can't imagine not setting my own rules!

**WHAT I LIKE LEAST ABOUT OWNING A BUSINESS:**

Being in control! It's a lot of responsibility!

**PEOPLE WOULD BE SURPRISED THAT I.**

Never went to design school.

**FAVORITE GUILTY PLEASURE SHOP-PING PLACE:**

Any high-end shoe store!

**PERSONAL TIME OFF INDULGENCE:**

Traveling the world over.

## Dema Grim

DEMA

1038 Valencia St.
415-206-0500
www.godemago.com

*"Never ignore your niche!"*

## 13. Living Room Events

958 Illinois St.  415-522-1417 (catering)
www.livingroomevents.com
Co-Owner: Kim Stevens
Living Room Events is a full-service caterer specializing in exquisitely crafted events where every detail is considered. Whether you want to pull off a sit-down dinner for 100 or a story-book wedding, the approach begins with your vision and culminates in an on-site experience that brings together all the elements of food, service, and style.

## 14. Mani Pedi

447 20th St.  415-401-MANI (pamper)
www.manipedi.com - Owner: Kelly Hensley
Nails. Toes. Wax. Tan. Relax. This award-winning nail spa opened in sunny Potrero Hill in 2001. They have received rave reviews from *InStyle*, *Lucky*, and *San Francisco* magazines, just to name a few. Cozy decor and friendly staff make this spot a "must do" on your list. Handbags, jewelry & accessories too.

## 15. Minnie Wilde

266 21st St.  415-642-9453 (boutique)
www.minniewilde.com
Owners: Terri Olson & Ann D'Apice
Triple the size of the original boutique, Minnie Wilde's home in the Mission carries the flirty yet edgy clothing line designed by owner Terri Olson, as well as other indie labels. Customers can slip inside the pink dressing room to try on one of the boutique's signature cropped bomber jackets—a must have for all devotees of San Francisco fashion.

## 16. Painted Bird

201A Guerrero St.  415-401-7027 (boutique)
www.paintedbird.org - Owner: Sunny Walker
Buy, sell, and trade vintage and contemporary clothing at this shop. Painted Bird offers you 35-percent cash or 55-percent in-store trade for any items it takes. Pop into the shop to get a feel of the merchandise. Men's and women's clothing, jewelry, bags, hats, shoes, reconstructed journals and clothing by owner Sunny Walker.

## 17. Porcelynne Boutique & Gallery

487 14th St.  415-310-8919 (boutique)
www.porcelynne.com - Owner: Jennifer Lynne
Check out one-of-a-kind lingerie and artwork all in
one trip. But don't be fooled; Porcelynne carries
much more than just lingerie—unique jewelry,
accessories, and clothing by local artisans can
also be found at this charming space. A bit off the
beaten path, it is certainly a gem of a find.

## 18. The Ribbonerie

191 Potrero Ave.  415-626-6184 (ribbons)
www.theribbonerie.com - Owner: Paulette Knight
The Ribbonerie is a unique specialty store featuring ribbons and trims from around the world.
Owner Paulette Knight was the original importer
of French wired ribbon to the United States.
Strictly wholesale for 12 years, she decided to
open this charming retail store nine years ago.
In addition, the shop features textile-related
antiques, button, laces, and vintage clothing.

## 19. stem

3690 18th St.  415-861-7836 (flowers)
www.stemsf.com - Owner: Maxine Siu
stem is an ever-changing store full of goodies for the home, accessories for men and
women, locally designed clothing for infant
and toddler, stationery, and jewelry. As if that
weren't enough, stem is also a full-service floral
boutique, delivering locally and nationwide to
weddings, restaurants, and residences. You can
even walk in and have your order filled.

## 20. Sunhee Moon

3167 16th St.  415-355-1800 (boutique)
www.sunheemoon.com
Designer/Owner: Sunhee Moon
Walk into this colorful boutique and be greeted
Izzy, the owner's Maltese, and frequently Sunhee
herself. Moon creates her designs on-site and ha
an aesthetic best defined as classic cuts with a
twist. Her line is complemented by fabulous han
bags, shoes, and locally designed jewelry. Salesgi
help you put it all together.

Currents

Parcelynne

Ribbonerie

Therapy

Virginia Howells

Sunhee Moon

## HOW MUCH MONEY DID IT TAKE TO START?

The profits from Hot! plus a loan from TMC Working Solutions for $25K, plus a loan from Jennifer's family for $10K was all it took.

## OUR ROLE MODELS/MENTORS:

Gwendolyn Wright from Renaissance Center for Entrepreneurship was instrumental in helping Jones craft her business plan and find lenders. Other role models included Jones' mom, Marilyn, and Klowden's dad, Bruce, for their support, hard work and can-do attitudes.

## ADVICE WE WOULD GIVE TO WOMEN STARTING THEIR OWN BUSINESS:

Partnership and collaboration are key. Your own business is hard work and requires a team to really pull it off without wearing yourself to the bone. Plus, it's way more fun to do it with friends.

## WHAT WE LIKE MOST ABOUT OWNING A BUSINESS:

Being part of our community and supporting a thriving neighborhood. Forging relationships with the many talented designers that we work with, and the inspiration that comes from them. Being creative and expressing ourselves through the creation of an experience for others. It's cool.

## WHAT WE LIKE LEAST ABOUT OWNING A BUSINESS:

Late, late nights, and eating at the same 5 restaurants on our street all of the time.

## PEOPLE WOULD BE SURPRISED THAT WE...

Work so many hours an never, ever feel caught up. People think retail is all fun and games, but that's the farthest thing from the truth. It's fun, but it's no game and it's hard work that requires a ton of dedication.

## FAVORITE GUILTY PLEASURE SHOPPING PLACE:

Adobe Books across the street.

# Jennifer Jones and Jenny Klowden

CANDYSTORE
3153 16th St.
415-863-8143
www.candystore-sf.com

""Inspired by the great gifts she found for friends while traveling in Europe, she decided to order small quantities of things to have a trunk show at her house. The next thing you know, she'd found a temporary storefront and opened a small boutique called Hot! in December 2004. Longtime friend Jenny Klowden came on as the vintage buyer for Hot!, and the beginnings of Candystore were born."

## 21. Therapy
545 Valencia St./541 Valencia St.
415-861-6213/415-621-5902 (décor)
Owner: Jing Chen; Manager: Maria Yen
Located in the heart of the sunny Mission, Therapy has been evolving for more than a decade but one thing remains constant: it's fun to shop here! There's a wonderful mix of men's and women's clothing, accessories, toys, and books. Next door, you'll find modern retro furniture and home accessories.

## 22. Virginia Howells
2839 24th St.  415-647-2082 (boutique)
www.howelltransmitter.com-Owner: Jennifer Welch
Be seduced by this tiny Mission boutique, indie record label, and vintage pulp fiction destination. It features an eclectic mix of vintage clothing, modern jewelry, and music that your collection desperately needs. Take home something from a jewelry designer from Kansas or psych-pop band that lives in the Mission. At Virginia Howells, bank on having a truly satisfying shopping experience.

Notes:

# NOE VALLEY

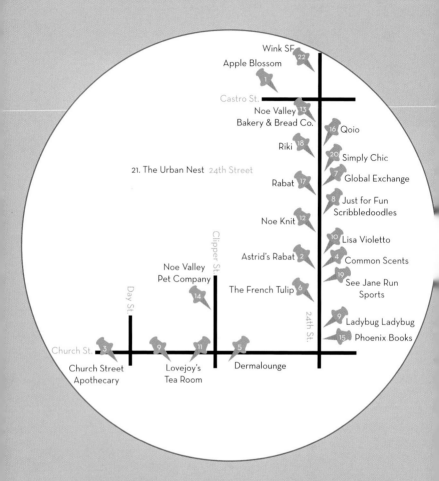

Wink SF 22

Apple Blossom

Castro St.

Noe Valley
Bakery & Bread Co. 13

16 Qoio

Riki 18

20 Simply Chic

21. The Urban Nest    24th Street

7 Global Exchange

Rabat 17

8 Just for Fun
Scribbledoodles

Noe Knit 12

10 Lisa Violetto

Astrid's Rabat 2

4 Common Scents

Clipper St.

19 See Jane Run
Sports

The French Tulip 6

Noe Valley
Pet Company

14

Day St.

9 Ladybug Ladybug

24th St.

15 Phoenix Books

Church St.   3

9   11   5

Church Street
Apothecary

Lovejoy's
Tea Room

Dermalounge

Relaxed and friendly residents make this neighborhood a must for gals browsing for ultra chic clothing, the latest sassy shoes or the coziest home decor. Pop by the local bookstore, sip an expresso & imbibe the local color of this enchanting enclave.

### 1. Apple Blossom

1303-C Castro St.   415-401-0602 (boutique)
Owner: Jin Kwon

Looking for unique design and great quality at a moderate price? Look no further than Apple Blossom. From unique bold graphic tees to feminine, lacy skirts, Apple Blossom carefully selects merchandise to complement a woman's ever-shifting mood. Also check out the one-of-kind, hand-stitched T-shirt collection made by owner/designer Jin Kwon.

### 2. Astrid's Rabat Shoes

3909 24th St.  415-282-7400 (shoes)
www.astrids-rabat-shoes.com
Manager: Veronica Ruedrich

Buyer/manager Veronica Ruedrich travels to the Las Vegas shoe show twice a year to handpick the freshest selection of European and domestic brands. She looks for exciting, comfortable, affordable footwear for men and women, not to mention strikingly distinctive socks and handbags. And—since 1977—the goods are served up by a friendly staff in a relaxed atmosphere.

### 3. Church Street Apothecary

1767 Church St.  415-970-9828 (gifts)
www.churchapothecary.com - Owner: Kati Kim

This neighborhood shop is your source for holistic, organic health and beauty products for the entire family. European shampoos share shelf space with handmade gifts, toys, books, and magazines. New parents find the natural baby care products (including organic diapers!) indispensable. You'll even find a few conventional brands beside homeopathic remedies, making this the local alternative to the "big box" stores!

### 4. Common Scents

3920 24th St., Suite A
415-826-1019 (scents)
Owners: Helen Norris & Linda Ramey

Since it first opened its doors in 1971, this cozy little store has been chock full of wonderful wares to pamper the face and body: imported French soaps, natural face care lines, aromatic essential oils, and luxurious bubble baths. If it's Kiehls, Dr. Hauschka, or Thymes products you crave, you'll have the "sense" to visit Common Scents!

The neighborhood was changing, and I thought The Urban Nest would make a perfect fit for the families that were moving here.

125K.

Be prepared to wear a lot of hats. It can feel overwhelming. Ask every expert you know to give you advice. Take it all in.

To under-buy for Christmas.

Being responsible for everything.

Being responsible for everything.

Have almost no retail experience.

Anthropologie.

Shopping for personal items.

# Heather Bruchs

THE URBAN NEST

3927 24th St.
415-341-0116

"The Urban Nest has been in operation for one year and has aught the neighborhood by storm. With in the few months of open-ing Daily Candy spotted us and eatured us. This brought on other ublications featuring us as well."

## Shel Mae Reinwald

GLOBAL EXCHANGE FAIR TRADE STORES

4018 24th Street
415-648-8068
www.globalexchangestore.org

"I am pleased to see a trend towards more women owned businesses. I believe that as a group we bring more compassion, humanity, and kindness into the business world... Plus, we rock."

### INSPIRATION/MOTIVATION FOR STARTING:

In The early 90s, I worked for Maya Traditions, a Fair Trade wholesale business, and traveling to Guatemala to meet our producer groups I was devastated by the poverty and desperation there. Maya Traditions has since formed 4 women's weaving groups, employing over 100 women. I saw the difference that a fair living wage made in these women's lives, and I committed myself to Fair Trade. I began managing Global Exchange's San Francisco store in 1998.

### HOW MUCH MONEY DID IT TAKE TO START?

My sister-in-law and I opened a Global Exchange store in Portland in 2003; we took out a $90,000 line of credit for remodeling and inventory. That was a lot of work. I think we were both tired for the next 6 months. We still owe on the loan. It seems like we need about that much money to keep us afloat during the year since over a third of our sales are in the last 3 weeks of the year.

### ADVICE I WOULD GIVE TO WOMEN STARTING THEIR OWN BUSINESS?

The best bosses are hands-on. Everyone would like to be a buyer, but for a small business like this one, its best to do a little of everything. One day I am meeting with delegates from Ghana, and the next I am cleaning the bathroom. Keep your finger on the pulse of the public, and engage wit and respect your employees. That's my advice.

### WHAT I LIKE MOST ABOUT RUNNING A BUSINESS:

Traveling and meeting the people who ben efit from our store, and the great feedbac and support we get from our community.

### PERSONAL TIME OFF INDULGENCE:

Adding to my waistline by conjuring up ne ways to cook the fabulous foods offered here in the Bay Area.

## 5. Dermalounge

1301 Church St.  415-285-6464 (pamper)
www.dermalounge.com - Owner: Nicole Alvino
Dermalounge is a sophisticated, sassy, and
revolutionary approach to skin health. Their skin
consultants design a personalized skin health program for each client to ensure glowing, healthy,
youthful skin. Dermalounge's team of skin-care
therapists and nurse practitioners offer facials,
waxing, chemical peels, microdermabrasion, laser
hair removal, IPL photorejuvenation, photody-
namic therapy, Botox, and Restylane.

## 6. The French Tulip

3903 24th St.  415-647-8661 (gifts)
www.frenchtulip.com - Owner: Laetitia Phelps
Known for low and lush bouquets as well as
French gifts for the home, the shop's products
bring a touch of France to your home. Before pur-
chasing the Tulip, Laetita and Daniel Phelps had a
shop in Bordeaux. But when they heard that this
flower shop—where they had met—was going to be
sold, they moved back and bought it.

## 7. Global Exchange Fair Trade Store

4018 24th St.  415-648-8068 (décor)
www.globalexchangestore.org
Manager: Shel Mae Reinwald
From handbags to housewares, Global Exchange
will inspire you with its fabulous selection of
handmade, fair trade treasures from the world's
artisans. Whether you are looking for textiles
from Asia, dishware from Tunisia or folk art from
Mexico, Global Exchange has an eclectic mix of
the work from the world's cooperatives and small,
family-owned businesses.

## 8. Just For Fun & Scribbledoodles

3982 24th St.  415-285-4068 (gifts)
www.justforfun.invitations.com
Manager: Raven Voss
Described as a "walk-in goodie bag" Just For Fun
is known for its unique gifts: from up-scale items to
gag-gifts and more. They also house Scribbledoodles, an in-store design/stationery center specializing in wedding invitations, birth announcements,
and all events in between. If you can't find the right
gift at Just For Fun, then it doesn't exist!

### 9. Ladybug Ladybug
3870 24th St.  415-824-5477 (gifts)
www.ladybugladybug.com
Owners: Lisa Sherratt & Sheila Isvanick
Ladybug Ladybug...send greetings home. This card boutique and gift shop is filled with lovely things to give and get. Discover an eclectic mix for kids, women, and men. While you're there, collect a stack of the best greeting cards in San Francisco. As an extra bonus, Ladybug Ladybug carries loads of local products.

### 10. Lisa Violetto
3932 24th St.  415-341-8442 (décor)
www.lisavioletto.com
Owners: Lisa Violetto & Judy Frangquist
Lisa Violetto is an accessories and gift store brimming over with goodies, including Lisa's own line of handmade bags, scarves, and jewelry. Customer favorites include Seda France candles, Gianna Rose Atelier Couture soaps, and vintage plaques from Moonlight & Roses. Owners Lisa and Judy both have backgrounds in art.

### 11. Lovejoy's Tea Room
1351 Church St.  415-648-5895 (eats)
www.lovejoystearoom.com
Owners: Gillian Briley & Muna Nash
Everyone at Lovejoy's invite you to sit back and enjoy the ritual of taking tea in a unique and unpretentious setting. The tearoom reflects the diversity of San Francisco, blending together the traditions of tea service with an eclectic, quirky, and playful spirit.

### 12. Noe Knit
3957 24th St.  415-970-9750 (knitting)
www.noeknit.com - Owner: Susan Herrick
This hip urban retreat blows the fusty "granny knitting store" image out of the water. With professional knitters and knitwear designers, a vast library and a brilliant, well-displayed selection, Noe Knit ushers in the new generation of knitters. More than a yarn store, Noe is inspiring, inviting, crisp and clean, and it will certainly get you hooked.

Apple Blossom

Astrid's

Common Scents

Global Exchange

Ladybug Ladybug

Lisa Violetto

## Susan Herrick

NOE KNIT

3957 24th St.
415-970-9750
www.noeknit.com

*"My store has departed a traditional 'retail' model, and has grown into a welcome gathering place. The line between customers and friends is now blurred."*

### INSPIRATION/MOTIVATION FOR STARTING MY BUSINESS:

I have always been an avid crafter. After a career in corporate training and team building, I decided that it was time to combine the creative element with the professional training. The classroom is an integral part of the store.

### HOW MUCH MONEY DID IT TAKE TO START?

A gut-wrenching, heart-stopping, breathlessly-brave amount of money.

### MY ROLE MODELS/MENTORS:

There are lots of people that helped to support me, especially in the beginning stages. My Aunt put me in touch with some friends of hers that had opened a store in Michigan. I created my own internship program, and worked with them for days. They remain a source of inspiration, ideas, and support.

### ADVICE I WOULD GIVE TO WOMEN STARTING THEIR OWN BUSINESS:

There are mentors everywhere. Seek help and advice from a wide variety of sources, then reflect, and use the information you can. Listen to the critics, they might bring up relevant obstacles. And then, be prepared to execute your plan despite them.

### PEOPLE WOULD BE SURPRISED THAT I

I did a stint as a comedienne "back in the day".

### FAVORITE GUILTY PLEASURE SHOPPING:

I love to go to antiquing. Several pieces I have collected are on display at the store.

**13. Noe Valley Bakery & Bread Co.**

4073 24th St.   415-550-1405 (eats)
www.noevalleybakery.com - Owner: Mary Gassen
Since it opened its doors in 1995, owners Mary
and Michael Gassen have dedicated themselves
to creating a small, independent, top-quality
neighborhood bakery. The ever-changing menu
of seasonal offerings reflects the bakery's passion
for bringing you what's fresh and what's best right
now. Planning a celebration?

**14. Noe Valley Pet Company**

451 Church St.  415-282-7385 (pets)
www.noevalleypet.com
Owners: Celia Sack & Paula Harris
The coolest cats and hippest dogs make their way
to Noe Valley Pet Company for the city's snazzi-
est collars, tastiest treats, and most mind-blowing
catnip. Antique pet store displays and plank floors
give the shop a general store feel. The store caters to everyone, so whether you want a $200 pet
tote or a 99-cent rawhide bone, you'll find it here.

**15. Phoenix Books**

3850 24th St.  415-821-3477 (books)
www.dogearedbooks.com/phoenix/index.htm
Owner: Kate Rosenberger
This fiercely independent bookstore carries
an eclectic collection of books, both new and
used. Alternately hip, nerdy, knowledgeable,
and warm, the store pays cash or trades for your
used books. If that wasn't enough, the shop is
dog friendly and encourages customers to bring
their pooches into the store.

**16. Qoio**

4068 24th St.  415-788-5566  (boutique)
www.qoio.com - Owner: Gilbertina Guarini
Focusing on world-inspired jewelry, native San
Franciscan's Gilbertina and Bruno Guarini have
created a truly enchanted feel in their shop.
Gilbertina is the artist and designer of all the
jewelry and creates pieces using an array of
colors and "no limit" designs. This is a one-of-a-
kind store with one-of-a-kind jewelry.

## 17. Rabat

4001 24th St.  415-282-7861 (shoes)
www.rabatshoes.com - Owner: Patricia Woody
A Noe Valley fixture for thirty-five years, this
friendly boutique specializes in limited-run,
hard-to-find European designers. Rabat offers
unique clothing, fashion-forward footwear, accessories, lingerie, and even a men's section for
boys to browse while the girls splurge on Robert
Clergerie, Cydwoq, Cop Copine, Nanette Lepore
Francesco Biasia, and Cosabella.

## 18. Riki

4037 24th St.  415-641-4407 (boutique)
www.rikidesign.com - Owner: Ursula Labermeier
Designer Ursula Labermeier brings together
classic cuts, luxurious fabrics, and unexpected
details to create the locally made Riki line that
fills this unique boutique. Alongside feminine,
European-inspired Riki pieces, find delicious
cashmere sweaters, trendsetting denim, the
perfect shoe for every outfit, and hand-crafted
jewelry. Riki gives new meaning to the phrase,
"one-stop shopping!"

## 19. See Jane Run Sports

3910 24th St.  415-401-8338 (boutique)
www.seejanerunsports.com-Owner: Lori Shannon
See Jane Run is where discerning women go to
get fit for running shoes. Besides offering gait
analysis, cutting-edge shoes, and up-to-date
wisdom, See Jane Run is a boutique full of
fashionable and functional athletic apparel.
You'll find running, yoga, and triathlon gear, and
sports bras for every shape and size. You now
have the tools for an active, stylish lifestyle.

## 20. Simply Chic

4028B 24th St.  415-550-6788 (boutique)
www.simplychicsf.com
Owner: Chuleemas Wichinrojjarun
This charming French boudoir dress shop ful-
fills your every elegant desire. Browse Simply
Chic's racks of gorgeous, colorful, detailed
dresses, whether you're a teen on the prowl
for the ultimate prom dress, or a mom in search
of something stylish. Simply Chic also stocks
ready-to-wear styles and lingerie, and with
home decor and gift sections coming soon.

Lovejoy's

Noe Valley Pet Co.

rabat

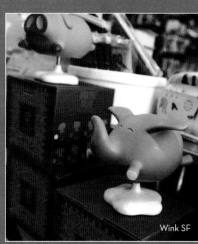
Wink SF

Qoio

The Urban Nest

ADVICE THAT WE WOULD GIVE TO WOMEN STARTING THEIR OWN BUSINESS:

Be aware that the first two years you may not earn an income, have a plan, be flexible work hard, do what it takes but don't let it take your life.

WHAT WE LIKE MOST ABOUT OWNING A BUSINESS IN SAN FRANCISCO:

The interaction with our local customers their children and pets!

WHERE WE LIKE TO INDULGE:

In the local coffee house – Martha's Coffee, and have mani's and pedi's whenever possible at National Nail right around the corner.

PEOPLE WOULD BE SURPRISED TO KNOW THAT...

Lisa and Sheila were both born in Californi (visit store to see what we mean).

## Lisa Sherratt & Sheila Isvanick

LADYBUG LADYBUG

3870 24th St.
415-824-5477
www.ladybugladybug.com

"Seeing daylight while at work and being part of a community where we know lots of first names is priceless."

### 21. The Urban Nest
3927 24th St.  415-341-0116 (décor)
Owner: Heather Bruchs
Locals flock to the Urban Nest for home furnishings, a perfect gift, or a personal indulgence that screams Paris chic or retro cool. The store is not only stunning but full of surprises. Heather Bruchs' keen eye delivers ever-changing merchandise that satisfies the romantic in all of us at prices that make it easy to splurge.

### 22. Wink SF
4107 24th Street  415-401-8881 (décor)
www.winksf.com
Owners: Teresa Hagiya & Marcy Israel
This colorful and eclectic store offers something for everyone. Owners Teresa and Marcy handpick the finest designer products, from bags and kitchen accessories to cards and toys. This fun Noe Valley shop specializes in unique and quirky items for the person who thinks she has everything. Highway bags, and angry girl bags and tees are customer favorites.

Notes:

# NORTH BEACH

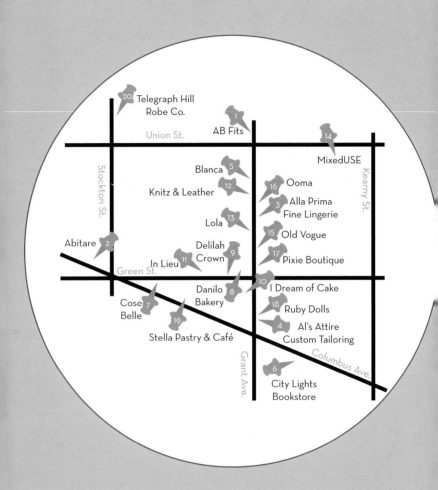

20. Telegraph Hill Robe Co.

Union St.

1. AB Fits

14. MixedUSE

Stockton St.

Kearny St.

5. Blanca

12. Knitz & Leather

16. Ooma

3. Alla Prima Fine Lingerie

13. Lola

15. Old Vogue

9. Delilah Crown

17. Pixie Boutique

2. Abitare

11. In Lieu

Green St.

10. I Dream of Cake

8. Danilo Bakery

7. Cose Belle

18. Ruby Dolls

19. Stella Pastry & Café

4. Al's Attire Custom Tailoring

Columbus Ave.

Grant Ave.

6. City Lights Bookstore

1. AB fits    2. Abitare

3. Alla Prima Fine Lingerie    4. Al's Attire Custom Tailoring

5. Blanca Café    6. City Lights Bookstore    7. Cose Belle    8. Danilo Bakery

9. Delilah Crown    10. I Dream of Cake    11. In Lieu    12. Knitz and Leather

13. Lola    14. mixedUSE    15. Old Vogue    16. ooma    17. Pixie Boutique

18. RubyDolls    19. Stella Pastry & Café    20. Telegraph Hill Robes

The Beat Generation has long since departed but the Bohemian vibe is here to stay. Old-school mom & pop stores dot the hilly streets and alleys, but a treasure trove ultra-chic & girly stores make Grant Street one of the City's fashion musts.

### 1. AB fits

1519 Grant Ave.   415-982-5726 (boutique)
www.abfits.com - Manager: Shannon Barnes
At AB fits North Beach, denim's the foundation for a wide range of street-smart fashions, both basic and not so basic. Tell your friends about it or just keep it as your little secret. The AB fits Union Square store offers plenty of denim as well but also carries clothes for fancier occasions, be it a wedding, hot date, or court appearance.

### 2. Abitare

522 Columbus Ave.   415-392-5800 (gifts)
Owner: Cia Van Orden
This gift boutique features a high-quality, eclectic variety of accessories for the home, bath, and kitchen, as well as a darling collection of children's toys and imported soft bears. Abitare also carries original paintings and sculpture by French artist Philippe Ferrari. Gifts include baskets from Indonesia and Mexico, lavender soap from France, beeswax candles, napkins and placemats, glassware, and decorative bowls.

### 3. Alla Prima Fine Lingerie

1420 Grant Ave.   415-397-4077 (lingerie)
Owners: Yolaida Duràn & Magie Crystal
Specializing in fine lingerie from Europe, including La Perla, and Eres, Alla Prima offers an inviting environment for women of all shapes and sizes, and is recognized nationally for attention to proper fit. They also carry hand-blended fragrances from DHS, swimwear with an eye to fashion and fit, and personal pleasure products from JimmyJane. (Also located in Hayes Valley.)

### 4. Al's Attire Custom Tailoring

1314 Grant Ave.   415-693-9900 (sewing)
www.homepage.mac.com/alsattire
Manager: Megumi Kusomoto
If you've got custom tailoring needs, head to Al's where you can have your pick of design, fabric, lining, and buttons. Al has deals with the best mills in Europe and the best cloth dealers in New York. He uses top-notch tailoring techniques and can take your sketch (along with your measurements) and produce a high-quality, perfect-fitting garment in a few weeks.

## Yolaida Durán & Magie Crystal

ALLA PRIMA FINE LINGERIE

1420 Grant Ave.
415-397-4077

"Yolaida saw a need and opportunity to provide women with a venue for high-end lingerie presented in an elegant yet modern environment that departed from the stereotypic boudoir model."

**OUR ROLE MODELS/MENTORS:**
Our greatest inspiration has been and continues to be found in small boutiques around the world that provide unique goods and services with a sense of pride.

**ADVICE WE WOULD GIVE TO WOMEN STARTING THEIR OWN BUSINES:**
Learn as much as you can about the every aspect of your business. Have a good business plan. Stay true to your vision especially when you encounter obstacles. Treat your staff with respect and kindness.

**MISTAKE THAT WE HOPE NOT TO REPEAT?**
Expanding so quickly we were not able to fully relish our success.

**WHAT WE LIKE MOST ABOUT OWNING OUR OWN BUSINESS:**
Being our own boss, of course! (Actually, we are pretty much bossed around by our staff).

**WHAT WE LIKE LEAST ABOUT OWNING OUR OWN BUSINESS:**
The fact that you can't blame the boss when things go wrong.

**PEOPLE WOULD BE SURPRISED THAT WE...**
**Magie:** love to watch cartoons.
**Yolaida:** write erotic short stories.

**FAVORITE GUILTY PLEAUSE SHOPPING:**
**Magie:** Bell'occhio on Brady Street in San Francisco because you're transported to a different world when you walk through the door. Everything is so finely edited and beautifully merchandised.
**Yolaida:** Guilt? What's that? I love visiting the apothecary at Santa Maria Novella in Florence.

**PERSONAL TIME OFF INDULGENCE:**
**Magie:** yoga, reading, visiting our wine country.
**Yolaida:** remodeling my 1903 Victorian flat.

## Shinmin Li

### I DREAM OF CAKE

1351 Grant Ave.
415-989-2253
www.idreamofcake.com

*"I've always loved art and cake. With a background in graphic design and patisserie, it was only natural to combine the two worlds of food and art. However I knew that no one is doing what I'm doing, bringing the level of cake design to such new heights, that I created a gallery to showcase my artwork."*

**HOW MUCH MONEY DID IT TAKE TO START?**
About $300,000

**MY ROLE MODELS/MENTORS:**
I've always admired Sylvia Weinstock and Colette Peters

**BEST ADVICE I RECEIVED BEFORE STARTING MY BUSINESS:**
Ironically, I received reversed advice from my mother. She doubted that this business could ever take off. She thought that I was making a huge mistake by chasing such a silly dream, so I set off to prove her wrong.

**MISTAKE THAT I HOPE NOT TO REPEAT**
Buying big time kitchen equipment without serious research. But who has the time?

**WHAT I LIKE MOST ABOUT OWNING A BUSINESS:**
Everything I do and see around me is a result of my own drive, passion, and love for art. Nothing pleases me more than seeing a client moved to tears because of my art.

**WHAT I LIKE LEAST ABOUT OWNING A BUSINESS:**
I work about 20 hours a day, 7 days a week

**PEOPLE WOULD BE SURPRISED THAT I**
Really love it when clients cut right into my cakes and devour the artwork that I've spent 60 hours creating. It's a completion of the art, and the taste is after all most important.

**FAVORITE GUILTY PLEASURE SHOPPING PLACE:**
I can spend hours at Sur La Table.

**PERSONAL TIME OFF INDULGENCE:**
Sleeping on my roof deck, and eating cashews.

## Blanca Café

141 Grant Ave.   415-291-9944 (eats)
www.blancacafe.com - Owner: Tanya Ristau
The concept: A Spanish-style wine bar and café
that pairs Andalusian fare with Spanish wine
and beer. The goal: To provide a relaxed, casual
atmosphere with great service where friends
and business associates can enjoy a glass of wine
and light fare. The result: A unique and satisfying
Spanish wining and dining experience.

## City Lights Bookstore

261 Columbus Ave.   415-362-8193 (books)
www.citylights.com - Manager: Elaine Katzenberger
Co-founded by poet/painter Lawrence Fer-
linghetti, City Lights is a landmark independent
bookstore and publisher that specializes in world
literature, the arts, and progressive politics. A
literary meeting place since 1953, City Lights
bookstore is one of the best general bookstores in
the U.S., internationally known for its expert selection and commitment to free intellectual inquiry.

## Cose Belle

60 Columbus Ave.   415-981-9470 (gifts)
Owner: Giulia D'Alo
Cose Belle Boutique, North Beach's newest
hotspot, represents gorgeous style, unique
variety, and high quality at exceptional prices.
Lose yourself in the eclectic collection of fabulous
fashions, delicious handbags, sassy shoes, and custom jewelry. If that weren't enough, Italian lingerie
and linens, luxurious bath products, home décor,
exciting imports, and gourmet condiments are all
here waiting for you.

## Danilo Bakery

516 Green St.   415-989-1806 (eats)
www.danilobakery.com
Co-Owner Stefania Gambaccini
Danilo Bakery has been a part of the Italian fabric
of the Beach. North Beach revelers have been
known to knock on the below-street-level bakery
door for an alcohol-absorbing late-night loaf of
bread, straight from the oven. Try their torta di
verdura, a slightly sweet little tart filled with finely
chopped Swiss chard, pine nuts and currants – a
spring specialty.

### 9. Delilah Crown

524 Green Street  415-765-9060 (boutique)
www.delilahcrown.com - Owner: Kristina De Pizzo
Nestled in the heart of North Beach amid biscott
bakeries and old time pizzerias you will find
the studio and retail space of Delilah Crown.
Enter into the bright, ethereal space created by
designer Kristina DePizzoc. Here you will find he
dreamy woman's collection, whimsical children's
clothing and pretty little things to make you smil

### 10. I Dream of Cake

1351 Grant Ave.  415-989-2253 (eats)
www.idreamofcake.com - Owner: Shinmin Li
Cakes are joyful centerpieces for all of life's
celebrations, including weddings, anniversaries,
birthdays, bar mitzvahs, and christenings. I Drear
of Cake designs and creates cakes that appeal t
the eye and most discerning palates—they are de
cious, moist, fluffy, and light. Owner Li's creation
are made from the highest quality ingredients ar
use only organic fruits.

### 11. In Lieu

528 Green St.  415-362-0202 (boutique)
www.inlieusf.com - Owner: Christina Claypool
Style mavens rush to this low-key boutique,
where seventies cool meets modern charm.
In Lieu stocks favorites from both established
and up-and-coming designers. Racks are filled
with adorable dresses by Corey Lynn Calter,
must-have pieces by Geren Ford, tops by Veena
Spring and Clifton, and of course a wide selectic
of designer denim, with brands such as Earnest
Sewn and Siwy.

### 12. Knitz and Leather

1429 Grant Ave.  415-391-3480 (boutique)
Owners: Katharina Ernst & Julia Relinghaus
This North Beach gem features handcrafted lea
jackets and one-of-a-kind knits that you can't fin
anywhere else. You can special order colors, sty
and sizes from German designers Katharina Ern
and Julia Relinghaus. The shop also carries an
unusual assortment of jewelry, leather bags, and
scarves. This is a true find.

Abitare

Alla Prima

Cose Belle

Delilah Crown

Dream of Cake

In lieu

## INSPIRATION/MOTIVATION FOR STARTING MY BUSINESS:

After spending 10 years as a Project Manager for various agencies, I was ready to manage my own "project". It became vital that I unleash my creativity into the world (and create a job that included shopping!)

## HOW MUCH MONEY DID IT TAKE TO START?

With a little elbow grease, a heave dose of creativity and lots of flea market excursion – about $50,000.

## MY ROLE MODELS/MENTORS:

From the shop owner where I worked prior to opening the store, to the reps that helped me with buying, to the designers who inspired me with their collections – an the Renaissance Entrepreneur Center – I received plenty of mentorship.

## ADVICE I WOULD GIVE TO WOMEN STARTING THEIR OWN BUSINESS:

It's easier than you think – just go for it!

## MISTAKE THAT I HOPE NOT TO REPEAT

When I started, many of the showrooms gave the impression that I should be placing orders at the showroom. Not knowing otherwise, I wrote up order after order – easily enticed by the shopping trip of my dreams. However – I ended up with many duplicates and buying things that were not quite right. Now, I look at everything first – then make my buying decisions in a more strategic fashion.

## WHAT I LIKE MOST ABOUT OWNING A BUSINESS:

The freedom to be creative and be in charge of my own life. It's the ultimate form of expression for me.

## WHAT I LIKE LEAST ABOUT OWNING A BUSINESS:

Filing – there is something about filing that I detest.

# Kate Logan

OOMA

1422 Grant Ave.
415-627-6963
www.ooma.net

*"I aim to support creativity, encourage self-expression, and have fun!"*

## 13. Lola

415 Grant Ave.  415-781-1817 (gifts)
www.lolaofnorthbeach.com - Owner: Amy Nanola
Lola is the kind of store where customers
are known to exclaim, "I can spend all day
here!" Find a refreshing selection of greeting
cards and stationery. Get organized with kolo
and russell+hazel. Indulge in aromatic candles.
The shop's baby gifts will be the hit of any baby
shower. For special occasions, drop in and design the perfect invitation or announcement.

## 14. mixedUSE

63 Union St.  415-956-1909 (boutique)
www.mixedusemodern.com
Owner: Katherine Johnstone
mixedUSE is a vintage mecca for fashion-forward
people who express their individuality in both
their home and personal style. Find everything
from vintage Chanel skirts and leather handbags
to Eames chairs and Lucite nesting tables. Owner
Johnstone stocks fashionable and modern pieces
that help make recycling a habit worth forming.

## 15. Old Vogue

412 Grant Ave.  415-392-1522 (boutique)
www.oldvogue.net - Owner: Michelle Nuelle
Old Vogue has been North Beach's secret since
1985, selling quality vintage clothing at reason-
able prices. Score a cashmere coat for $150 or
cashmere sweater for $45. Specializing in men's
clothing, the store is loaded with shirts, suits, and
sport coats from the 1940s, 50s and 60s, as well
as hundreds of Levi 501 jeans.

## 16. ooma

22 Grant Ave.  415-627-6963 (boutique)
www.ooma.net - Owner: Kate Logan
ooma celebrates individual style. The boutique is
aware of trends and often sets a few, but wants its
customers not to look like everyone else. Owner
Logan believes in accessories and their ability to
transform an outfit. Naturally, the jewelry selection
is extensive and includes unique yet totally wear-
able pieces. The dresses seduce, the tops charm,
and the skirts flirt.

## 17. Pixie Boutique
1400 Grant Ave.  415-392-1090 (boutique)
www.pixieboutique.com
Owners: Amy Newman & Carol Wu
Come inside Pixie and find everything a girl can imagine—denim that fits and complements every curve, dresses for a wedding or evening event, tops that make you feel so sexy it's almost impossible to leave wearing your original clothes, and accessories featuring one-of-a-kind belts and locally designed baubles.

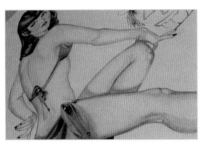

## 18. RubyDolls
1318 Grant Ave.  415-834-9762 (boutique)
www.rubygirl.com - Owner: Ruby Hadley
Fun, frisky, fantasy fashions are available at RubyDolls exotic boutique. The store is filled with a variety of ladies' clothing like dresses, shirts, and jackets, plus hats, handbags, scarves, sunglasses, and costume jewelry, all with affordable price tags. The owner's own line of handmade risqué Rubygirl lingerie is popular with local models and exotic dancers.

## 19. Stella Pastry & Café
446 Columbus Ave.  415-986-2914 (eats)
www.stellapastry.com
Owners: Christina & Silvia Santucci
STELLA! You'll be shouting that too after you try the bakery's intoxicating desserts and coffees. The selection of traditional Italian cookies and pastries will astound you, but don't pass up the patented Sacripantina, the house specialty and a favorite among locals and travelers alike. Enjoy the ambience of a North Beach institution that's been around for more than 60 years.

## 20. Telegraph Hill Robes
1706 Stockton St.  415-398-7010 (boutique)
www.telegraphhill.com - Owner: Maria Spurlock
Like their San Franciscan namesake, Telegraph Hill bathrobes make wearers feel on top of the world. Telegraph Hill supplies bathrobes and spa wraps to some of the nation's most exclusive spas and resorts, including Auberge Du Soleil, Ojai Valley Inn & Spa, and Elizabeth Arden Red Door Spas. Now, the company would like to bring the spa to your front door.

Lola

mixedUSE

Old Vogue

Pixie

Stella Pastry

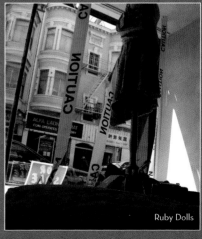

Ruby Dolls

**ADVICE I WOULD GIVE TO WOMEN STARTING THEIR OWN BUSINESS:**

Invest your own time and money. Listen to your gut.

**MISTAKE THAT I HOPE NOT TO REPEAT:**

I see mistakes as learning experiences – they are part of life. Don't sweat the small stuff.

**WHAT I LIKE MOST ABOUT OWNING A BUSINESS:**

Meeting people. I love getting to know the people who walk through the door.

**PERSONAL TIME OFF INDULGENCE:**

Buying flowers – it always puts me in a goo mood.

## Kristina De Pizzol

DELILAH CROWN

524 Green Street
415-765-9060
www.delilahcrown.com

"I love to dream up new designs
and see people get excited about
them. I love to play with color and
fabric – it is always fresh
and exciting."

Notes:

# PACIFIC HEIGHTS/UPPER FILLMORE

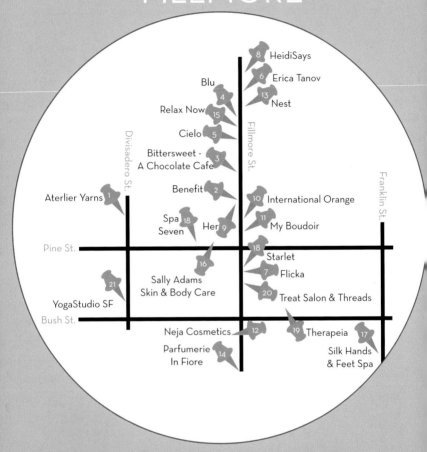

8 HeidiSays
6 Erica Tanov
Blu
4
13 Nest
Relax Now
15
Cielo
5
Bittersweet -
A Chocolate Cafe
3
Benefit
2
10 International Orange
Aterlier Yarns 1
11 My Boudoir
Spa 18
Seven    Her 9
18 Starlet
16
7 Flicka
Sally Adams
Skin & Body Care
20 Treat Salon & Threads
21
YogaStudio SF
Neja Cosmetics 12    19 Therapeia
Parfumerie
In Fiore                                              17
14                              Silk Hands
& Feet Spa

Divisadero St.    Fillmore St.    Franklin St.
Pine St.
Bush St.

1. Atelier Yarns   2. Benefit Cosmetics
3. Bittersweet: The Chocolate Café   4. Blu   5. Cielo   6. Erica Tanov
7. Flicka   8. HeidiSays   9. Her   10. International Orange
11. My Boudoir Lingerie   12. Neja Cosmetics   13. Nest
14. Parfumerie In Fiore   15. Relax Now   16. Sally Adams Skin & Body Care
17. Silk Hands & Feet Spa   18. Starlet   19. Therapeia
20. Treat Salon & Threads   21. YogaStudio SF

*Victorians and Mansions dot this moneyed hilltop community where the beautiful people mix and mingle at the many ritzy retailers & restaurants. Grab your Vanity Fair and rest your tootsies while you people watch at Washington Square Park.*

### 1. Atelier Yarns

1945 Divisadero St.  415-771-1550 (knitting)
www.atelieryarns.com
Owners: Grace & Chaele Cooper
Stocked floor to ceiling with gorgeous yarns and knitting accessories from around the world, Atelier Yarns has been a destination for experienced knitters and novices for 15 years. Mother–daughter co-owners offer a friendly, fashion-forward haven for everyone with a passion for or curiosity about knitting and crochet. Specialties include hand-dyed gems, natural fibers, and classes.

### 2. Benefit Cosmetics

2117 Fillmore St.  415-567-0242 (pamper)
www.benefitcosmetics.com
Owners: Jean & Jane Ford
Creative products, hysterical names, and a fun atmosphere attract women from around the world to Benefit. Since 1976, Benefit has set itself apart with its original line of "fake-its," little look-goods that instantly correct pesky beauty flaws. Quality products—including makeup, skincare, and bodycare collections, intriguing packaging, and lots of laughter—make Benefit the most action-packed brand in the business.

### 3. Bittersweet: The Chocolate Café

2123 Fillmore St.  415-346-8715 (eats)
www.bittersweetchocolatecafe.com
Owners: Penelope Finnie, Beth & Bonnie Rostan
Step into this chocolate oasis and enjoy one of seven mood-elevating hot chocolates with a yummy homemade pastry. Or choose from more than 125 chocolate bars from the world's top chocolatiers. Whether you are a milk, dark, or exotic chocolate girl (A chocolate absinthe bar, perhaps? How about chocolate Thai iced tea?), Bittersweet will satisfy your sweet tooth.

### 4. Blu

2259 Fillmore St.  415-776-0643 (boutique)
Owner: Merhi Jaiswal
Blu boutique is the destination for those who seek style and new ideas. The store is designed by renowned architect Aston Pereira, who has created a modern space with circular dressing rooms, concrete floor, and unique lighting. The store carries eclectic fashions from around the world such as Y's, Vanessa Bruno, Marithé & François Girbaud, and Barbara Bui.

## Jean & Jane Ford

BENEFIT COSMETICS

2117 Fillmore St.
415-567-0242
www.benefitcosmetics.com

"We wanted to be shopkeepers because we love working with people, and knew when we started Benefit that we would either sell makeup or casseroles. We literally flipped a coin to decide which type a store to open. We love both, so it was a hard decision to make. We're happy to be in makeup, there is nothing better to make you smile and feel good!"

### MY ROLE MODELS/MENTORS:

Our mother and grandmother are our role models. We were lucky to always have them around and still to this day to give us advice and someone to lean on for support.

### ADVICE THAT WE WOULD GIVE TO WOMEN STARTING THEIR OWN BUSINESS:

**Jean Ford:** My advice would be to have passion and believe in yourself. If you don't believe in yourself, no one else will believe in you.
**Jane Ford:** Work hard and be on time. It's important to have tenacity. Never give up

### WHAT WE LIKE MOST ABOUT OWNING A BUSINESS:

Working with our amazing team of talented people who keep Benefit on top of the game!

### PEOPLE WOULD BE SURPRISED THAT I...

**Jean Ford:** Love to swing on the swings at the park, it helps me think.

### FAVORITE GUILTY PLEASURE SHOPPING:

Neiman Marcus in Union Square, definitely!

### PERSONAL TIME OFF INDULGENCE:

**Jean Ford:** Hanging with my two daughters and going to the spa.
**Jane Ford:** Hanging out with my nieces and going to my pilates class!

## Judy Gilman & Marcella Madsen

NEST

2300 Fillmore St.
415-292-6199

"Do something you have a personal passion for."

**INSPIRRATION/MOTIVATION FOR STARTING OUR BUSINESS:**

To justify our love of travel.

**HOW MUCH MONEY DID IT TAKE TO START?**

More than money, it takes experience and the right location.

**MY ROLE MODEL/MENTOR:**

Dalai Lama.

**MISTAKE THAT I HOPE NOT TO REPEAT?**

Locking Sharon Stone in the bathroom.

**WHAT I LIKE MOST ABOUT OWNING A BUSINESS:**

Freedom – I love doing exactly what I want to do!

**WHAT I LIKE LEAST ABOUT OWNING A BUSINESS:**

The business part.

**PEOPLE WOULD BE SURPRISED THAT..**

I am not a millionaire.

**FAVORITE GUILTY PLEASURE SHOPPING PLACE:**

John Derian store in NYC.

## 5. Cielo

2225 Fillmore St.  415-776-0641 (boutique)
Owners: Merhi Jaiswal

Cielo carries designer clothing at the forefront of the international fashion scene. Dries Van Noten, Ann Demeulemeester, Yohji Yamamoto, Anne Valérie Hash, Zucca, Tsumori Chisato, and others draw celebrities and people in the know. The modern, spacious store has a 16-foot-high ceiling, which complements the designer clothes and allows customers to be inspired.

## 6. Erica Tanov

1408 Fillmore St.  415-674-1228 (boutique)
www.ericatanov.com - Owner: Erica Tanov

Subtle. Soft. Beautiful. Clean. Pure. There is a thread that runs through everything Erica Tanov does, whether it's her women's wear collection, her bed linens, the children's clothing line, or the serenity she creates in her stores. Reminiscent of vintage lingerie, Tanov's delicate silk tops, skirts, and dresses are perfect for layering with tunics, knit skirts, and cardigans.

## 7. Flicka

1932 Fillmore St.  415-292-2315 (boutique)
www.flickaboutique.com
Owners: Malin Leschly & Catarina Norman

Flicka showcases Scandinavian lifestyle with a variety of women's fashion and design items. The shop's products meld a clean, simple look with a fashion edge and it carries designers who embody the trendy-yet-timeless Scandinavian ideal. The boutique is a cool, comfortable and inviting place of creamy whites, dark wood, and sky blue accents.

## 8. HeidiSays

2426 Fillmore St.  415-749-0655 (boutique)
www.heidisays.com - Owner: Heidi Sabelhaus

HeidiSays features clothing, shoes, and accessories from up-and-coming fashion designers, as well as tried-and-true boutique designers who never disappoint. At HeidiSays, we specialize in pleasing all types of fashionistas, with sporty and tailored Theory pants, fabulous dresses from Diane Von Furstenberg and M Missoni, and the latest denim. HeidiSays has what you want (if not need).

# Pacific Heights/Upper Fillmore

## 9. Her
2053 Fillmore Street  415-923-9628 (boutique)
www.her-sf.com - Owner: Tonya Milteer
HER boutique gives "media-darling" designers center-stage. HER cherry-picks styles from the designer collections most favored by fashion publications like *InStyle*, *Elle* and *Vogue*. Busy moms stop in for the newest Lily McNeal sweaters, Vince trousers, Zooey tees, and denim by Paige Premium. Young fashionistas make frequent appearances.

## 10. International Orange
2044 Fillmore St.  415-563-5000 (pamper)
www.internationalorange.com-Owners: Amy Darland, Melissa Ferst & Kary Chendo
Since May 2002, International Orange (IO) has specialized in expert, transformative, and nurturing massage; organic, results-oriented skincare; and invigorating, body-altering yoga. It's all in the details at IO: warm towels are infused with essential oils, eye pads are soaked in cucumber water, and delicate flowers float below the face cradle of massage tables.

## 11. My Boudoir Lingerie
2029 Fillmore St.  415-346-1502 (lingerie)
www.myboudoir.net
Owner: Geraldine Moreno Nuval
Step inside this intimate boutique, where colorful European lingerie adorns the shabby chic interior, luxurious silks slide through your fingers, and the scent of French hard-milled soaps and candles fill the air. My Boudoir carries intimate apparel for your ever-changing moods—sweet, sexy, seductive, and simple.

## 12. Neja Cosmetics
1850 Fillmore St.  415-345-8301 (makeup)
www.nejacosmetics.com-Owner: Nellie Muganda
One of the country's most sought-after makeup artists, Nellie Muganda opened Neja Cosmetics in 1990 after 20 years of flying coast to coast for fashion shows, Vogue covers, and TV commercials. Today, Bay Area brides, businesswomen, and celebrities trust Neja to give them the ideal look for an important occasion. Neja custom-blends cosmetics and offers facials, hair styling, and waxing.

The legend of

Long ago, in this ver...

No...wait...two babies.

And as the twins grew,

The one known as...

Benefit Cosmetics

Cielo

Brice Tondo

HeidiSays

In Fiore

International Orange

## HOW MUCH MONEY DID IT TAKE TO START?
$750K all in.

## ROLE MODELS/MENTORS:
Marcia Kilgore of Bliss was our business idol as young professionals in NYC. Spiritual role model is Jack Kornfield from Spirit Rock. Female role models are our moms who are both independent, productive, strong and creative. Mentors were many. We took ALL the advice we could get and still do.

## ADVICE WE WOULD GIVE TO WOMEN STARTING THEIR OWN BUSINESS:
A healthy dose of naiveté helps keep the ball rolling with a new business, a first business especially, when the work is pretty much endless and potentially much more complicated than expected. Partnership can be though, but can also be a lifesaver. Make sure you very clearly iron out expectations, duties, and compensation. It might seem tedious or overboard, but in the end it will help clarify roles and minimize confusion... Have a clear vision. Put it all down on paper. Then be flexible with that original concept so you can still allow it to grow and transform.

## WHAT WE LIKE MOST ABOUT OWNING A BUSINESS:
Feeling proud of having created a space that really communicates a special environment, and of the community we have created with our staff and clients. We are very fortunate and we work hard for it. Usually we practice what we preach and that feels so good.

## WHAT WE LIKE LEAST ABOUT OWNING A BUSINESS:
Sometimes it makes you want to grab the mane of a wild horse and ride as far away from all the little headaches and responsibility and toward freedom and solitude.

# Amy Darland, Melissa Ferst & Kary Chendo

### INTERNATIONAL ORANGE

2044 Fillmore St.
415-563-5000
www.internationalorange.com

*"We ventured into the endeavor of creating what we dreamed of as the an elegant, real, friendly, intentional wellness community that is one part spa, one part yoga, one part amazing retail boutique and one part lounging space."*

## 3. Nest

2300 Fillmore St.  415-292-6199 (boutique)
Owners: Judy Gilman & Marcella Madsen
You'll feel right at home in this cozy, bohemian
den. Formerly a Victorian-era pharmacy, Nest is
now a lovely home-accessories store with wire
chandeliers, high ceilings, and rustic French props.
Mother and daughter Judy Gilman and Marcella
Madsen have created an enchanting shopping
atmosphere, with Italian hand-blocked quilts, John
Derian decoupage plates, embroidered coats,
French toys, and Moroccan poufs.

## 4. Parfumerie In Fiore

Harputs Market  1525 Fillmore St.
415-922-9644 (scents)
Owner: Julie Elliott
In Fiore was born by inspired and exhaustive
research of European apothecaries and their
historic methods of crafting beauty products.
The parfumerie showcases owner Elliott's
favorite fragrances from Paris and her own
custom-blended scents, skincare, and body
care lines.

## 5. Relax Now

241 Fillmore St.  415-56-RELAX (pamper)
www.relaxnow.net - CEO: Leslie Villarreal
This day spa can't wait to spoil you rotten.
Famous for combining pampering services with a
striking décor, Relax Now features state-of-the-
art skin care and a dazzling menu of "result-
oriented" facial treatments. Don't leave with
out trying Relax's signature skincare line, which
beauty editors are buzzing about. Visit the website to purchase products and gift certificates, or
send a free e-card.

## 6. Sally Adams Skin & Body Care

258 Pine Street  415-775-6546 (pamper)
www.sallyadamsdayspa.com - Owner: Sally Adams
Sally Adams Skin & Body Care specializes in
pampering mind, body and spirit. Each signature
treatment—from luxurious facials to deep, healing
massages—is tailored to you. Sally Adams provides
a comfortable, low-key environment. You feel
like you're going to a girlfriend's house—if that
girlfriend gave expert massages and facials that
would leave you feeling and looking like a million
bucks.

**17. Silk Hands & Feet Spa**
1425 Franklin St.  415-885-3277 (pamper)
www.silkhandsandfeetspaa.com
Owner: J. Chang
The moment you step through the doorway, Silk aims to engage all your senses, not just groom your hands and feet. Have a beverage, nibble on some sweets, and choose from the shop's designer polishes. Try the signature pedicure: your feet soak in a pool of lavender petals, are wrapped in hot towels, and are then massaged with warm lotion.

**18. Starlet**
1942 Fillmore St.  415-440-3550 (bridal)
Owner: Allison Hargrave
This boutique is filled with glamorous gowns and dresses designed by Badgley Mischka Tadashi, Dolce Jovani, and Nicole Miller. Starlet also has over-the-top jewelry and accessories, including handbags by Mary Francis and Debbie Brooks. The store is filled with crystal chandeliers, vintage artwork from the 1930s, and knowledge-able sales associates that can help you find the perfect outfit for any occasion.

**19. Therapeia**
1801 Bush St.  415-885-4450 (pamper)
www.therapeiaspa.com - Owner: Lauri Karstetter
Therapeia's goal is to help people relax, rejuve-nate, and feel great. Skilled therapists use heal-ing hands to provide you with an experience that improves your well-being from the inside out. The spa practices integrative therapeutic health and offers specialized treatments for the body, including endermologie and acupuncture.

**20. Treat Salon & Threads**
1928 Fillmore St.  415-567-0166 (pamper)
www.treatsf.com - Owner: Tammy Redsun
Treat has everything that modern girls crave. Every service at Treat, the city's flagship Aveda salon, starts when you sit down and place your feet in an aromatherapy foot bath while you receive a hand massage. Treat specializes in European haircutting, natural blonde highlights, and great blowouts. Treat Threads features European designers, sexy jeans, high-quality basics, great handbags, and hip belts.

In Fiore

Neja

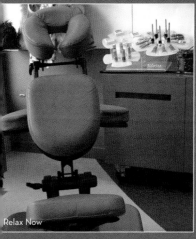

Relax Now

Starlet

Treat

Blu

## Heidi Sabelhaus

HEIDISAYS

2426 Fillmore St.
415-749-0655
www.heidisays.com

"It's more about style for me than fashion.
I appreciate lots of different looks; tailored,
bohemian, romantic but more importantly,
I appreciate the style and creativity of the
individual... Sure I appreciate and indulge
in trends, that's how I make a living, but
there's nothing like a woman strutting her
style with a combination of pieces that have
been in her closet for years mixed with one
brand new up to date piece. That's style,
not fashion."

### INSPIRATION/MOTIVATION FOR START-ING MY OWN BUSINESS:

It was always a dream of mine as it is for many women. I knew there were enough people who appreciated my style and my unwavering interest in fashion and the art of design inspired me to open HeidiSays. Also, I typically found that I had to shop at too many different stores to get the right recipe of style that I desired, so I wanted to open an all-encompassing store like the one that I wished I could shop in.

### MY BACKGROUND/HISTORY/EDUCA-TION:

I graduated from Gonzaga University with a major in Art History and a minor in Business. I spent one year of College studying Art History in Florence, Italy. After graduation I moved to San Francisco to work for a large local art dealer. I then moved into the world of advertising working closely with the CKS design team on several different creative projects with clients including Pixar and Nike.

### MY FASHION ROLE MODELS/MENTOR:

My own group of discerning, discriminating fashionista friends and my metrosexual guy buddies who will always tell me the truth! I also keenly observe the fashion savvy women who respect and admire the style that HeidiSays portrays. She's a woman who isn't of a specific age but who has a specific style. She's sophisticated, chic and likes to dip into a few of the seasonal trends.

### MY FASHION ADVICE:

Don't be a sheep. We are so tempted to copy one another. This movement is making fashion in America very repetitive and dull. If you like being a trend follower, branch out, try something different with your combinations and make your own statement. If you don't feel comfortable following trends, find the style that suits you best. If you look fabulous in tailored clothing, don't buy a negligee top just because it's trendy.

## 21. YogaStudio SF
1823 Divisadero St. 415-292-5600 (yoga)
www.yogastudiosanfrancisco.com
Owner: Joan Barnes

YogaStudio SF's new 5,000-square-foot studio offers a peaceful, luxurious ambience, a revitalizing, nurturing community, and a stylish yoga boutique. The studio offers more than 75 classes, spanning experience levels and yoga lineages. It has "concierges" who can pair the correct classes and teachers with each practitioner; spa-like amenities; an exquisite, extensive boutique; and an exclusive series of yoga retreats.

Notes:

# PRESIDIO HEIGHTS

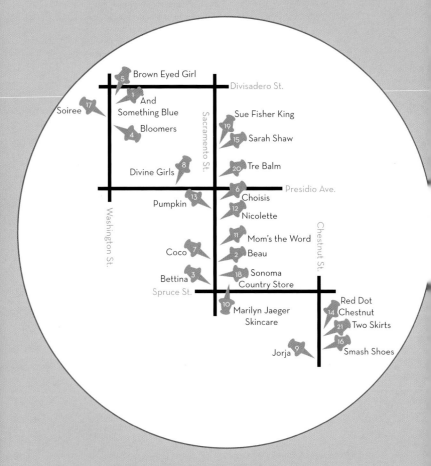

Brown Eyed Girl
Divisadero St.
And Something Blue
Soiree
Bloomers
Sue Fisher King
Sarah Shaw
Sacramento St.
Tre Balm
Divine Girls
Presidio Ave.
Pumpkin
Choisis
Nicolette
Mom's the Word
Coco
Beau
Bettina
Sonoma Country Store
Spruce St.
Washington St.
Chestnut St.
Marilyn Jaeger Skincare
Red Dot
Chestnut
Two Skirts
Smash Shoes
Jorja

1. And Something Blue   2. Beau
3. Bettina   4. bloomers   5. Brown Eyed Girl   6. Choisis
7. COCO A-Mist Tanning Boutique   8. Divine Girls   9. Jorja
10. Marilyn Jaeger Skincare   11. Mom's The Word   12. Nicolette
13. Pumpkin, Hip Clothes for Cool Babes   14. Red Dot   15. Sarah Shaw
16. Smash Shoes   17. Soirée San Francisco   18. Sonoma Country Store
19. Sue Fisher King   20. Tre Balm   21. Two Skirts

Compare and contrast these two neighborhoods and you couldn't find more contradictions. Presidio Heights & Sacramento Street ladies scream sophistication, while Chestnut Street Marina Girls emanate a sexy, sporty style.

### 1. And Something Blue

2999 1/2 Washington St.  415-409-0217 (bridal)
www.shopbrowneyedgirl.com-Owner: Danielle Bouhris
By offering less-traditional dresses, And Something Blue is a godsend for hordes of stressed-out brides-to-be and their bridesmaids. And Something Blue is filled with fabulous frocks for the wedding party, along with a selection of bridal accessories and gifts. Knowing that many women don't fit the cookie-cutter mold, the shop stocks dresses that are beachy casual, romantic, trendy, and traditional.

### 2. Beau

3571 Sacramento St.  415-440-1058 (boutique)
www.beauboutique.com - Owner: Brooke Read
Beau is a high-end women's boutique in San Francisco that carries lines like Tory by TRB, Lela Ross, Vena Cava, Paul & Joe, and Catherine Malandrino among many others. It features jewelry, handbags by Rebecca Minkoff and Botkier, and high-end jeans such as Sass & Bide. You don't want to miss this special hidden boutique in the residential area of Pacific Heights.

### 3. Bettina

3654 Sacramento St.  415-563-8002 (boutique)
www.bettinasf.com - Owner: Doretta Boehm
Be drawn in first by chic visuals of contemporary design and let the experience unfold in the warm inviting atmosphere of Bettina. Browse the fabulous selection of ornate jewelry and handbags from local design talents. Try on clothing from established lines: fun and flirty styles from L.A. to cutting-edge refined looks from New York.

### 4. bloomers

2975 Washington St  415-563-3266 (flowers)
Manager: Kelley Dillon
Established in 1977, this charming neighborhood shop specializes in garden style arrangements and simple unconstructed compositions. Daily trips to local growers and wholesalers allow the shop to offer a superb selection of premium seasonal flowers and exotic orchid plants. An extensive selection of vases, baskets, and containers is always available. City-wide delivery.

## Sue Fisher King

SUE FISHER KING

3067 Sacramento St.
415-922-7276

"Sue Fisher King opened in
1978 with the same purpose that
we are still fulfilling today — to
bring interesting discoveries in home
design to the customers who want
to be enticed and informed on the
latest trends."

**INSPIRATION/MOTIVATION FOR STARTING MY BUSINESS:**
I had a lot of ideas that I wanted to realize.

**HOW MUCH MONEY DID IT TAKE TO START?**
$300,000 – including remodeling.

**MY ROLE MODELS/MENTORS:**
I had a terrific, creative boss at I. Magnin who had wonderful sources in Europe, and also a great way of combining products. Jacques Neuville – he was a role model.

**ADVICE I WOULD GIVE TO WOMEN STARTING THEIR OWN BUSINESS:**
Be sure you are not under capitalized; that you have the most savvy people giving you advice; that you realize you cannot be good at everything and must delegate.

**MISTAKE THAT I HOPE NOT TO REPEAT:**
Hiring people who are not right for my business, and then not knowing how (or being unwilling) to tell them.

**WHAT I LIKE MOST ABOUT OWNING A BUSINESS:**
The freedom to be as creative as you feel, pursuing any direction that beckons.

**WHAT I LIKE LEAST ABOUT OWNING A BUSINESS:**
Trying to coax reluctant suppliers to make your orders and ship them – especially after they have your money.

**PEOPLE WOULD BE SURPISED THAT I...**
Love babies and dogs.

**FAVORITE GUILTY PLEASURE SHOPPING PLACE:**
Hermès – a rare but exhilarating experience!

**PERSONAL TIME OFF INDULGENCE:**
Eating ice cream, watching The Daily Show, and playing board games on Pogo.com.

## Marilyn Jaeger

MARILYN JAEGER SKINCARE

3384 Sacramento St.
415-751-0647
www.marilynjaegerskincare.com

As the company's founder, Marilyn Jaeger formulated her own product – "spotless potion for ingrown hairs". Her second location in Eastbay 5257 College Avenue).

### INSPIRATION/MOTIVATION FOR STARTING MY BUSINESS:
My devotion to making a difference in peoples lives. My way of seeing beauty in everyone and sharing with them so they can feel beautiful too!

### HOW MUCH MONEY DID IT TAKE TO START?
It took a lot of tenaciousness and perseverance. I had very little capital and a whole lot of sweat equity.

### MY ROLE MODEL/MENTOR:
One special one – Anastasia "Brow Guru to the Stars", is a friend and was a huge inspiration for me to trade in my pastry bag for tweezers, 15 years ago.

### ADVICE I WOULD GIVE TO WOMEN STARTING THEIR OWN BUSINESS:
Be prepared to raise it like a child. 100% priority, when it's hungry, feed it. When it cries you hold it and nurture it into full maturity. It takes a lot of dedication and time.

### MISTAKE THAT I HOPE NOT TO REPEAT
Taking things too personally.

### WHAT I LIKE MOST ABOUT OWNING A BUSINESS:
I love my clients and my employees – they are all very diverse and make my life a colorful place!

### PEOPLE WOULD BE SURPRISED THAT
Was raised in socially vulnerable circumstances and have built my empire solo from the ground up.

### FAVORITE GUILTY PLEASURE SHOPPING PLACE:
Buenos Aires, Argentina.

### PERSONAL TIME OFF INDULGENCE:
Men – tee hee.

## Brown Eyed Girl

999 Washington St.  415-409-0214 (boutique)
www.shopbrowneyedgirl.com
Owner: Danielle Bouhris
Everything about this store, housed in an adorable
Victorian flat, makes shoppers feel as if they are
hanging out in their best-dressed friend's closet.
Owner brown-eyed Danielle Bourhis has created
a comfortable haven for women to shop, chat, and
bond, and filled it with flirty and feminine frocks,
sizzling denim, and gobs of girlie gifts, accessories,
and furniture.

## Choisis

3350 Sacramento St.  415-673-8388 (boutique)
Owner: Chiaki Kasatani
This chic boutique celebrates the refined sensibili-
ties of Kyoto and the stylish inclinations of Paris.
Choisis showcases the collections of rare and
diverse European and Asian designers. From the
avant-garde refinement of Karl Lagerfeld to the
cosmopolitan elegance of Sophie Hong, Choisis
presents sophisticated choices for the discerning
woman.

## COCO A-Mist Tanning Boutique

3516 Sacramento St.  415-771-2244 (pamper)
www.cocoboutique.com
COCO is San Francisco's premier tanning
boutique, bringing you the latest in mist tanning
technology. When you visit COCO, step into a
private booth and be sprayed with a refreshing
mist for about 45 seconds. The result is a golden-
brown tan that will leave your skin looking beautiful. Maintain a gorgeous tan all year round without
worrying about harmful UV rays.

## Divine Girls

40 Presidio Ave.  415-409-4901 (boutique)
www.divinegirls.net - Owner: Maria Muzio
Divine Girls is a boutique catering to discerning,
fashionable women of all ages. From the simplest
jeans and tees to the most extraordinary cocktail
dress, there is always something to swoon over at
this chic store. The friendly, knowledgeable staff is
just one more reason that Divine Girls is the coolest shopping experience in town.

## 9. Jorja

2015 Chestnut St.  415-674-1131 (boutique)
Owner: Jorja Gaskins

Whether it's a casual date or a black tie affair, Jorja is the ideal boutique to find the perfect ensemble to dress to impress. Blushing brides and bridesmaids who'd rather look hip and haute can special order their dream dresses and accessorize with fabulous shoes, purses, wraps, and jewelry. Stop by Jorja for all your day to evening shopping needs.

## 10. Marilyn Jaeger Skincare

3384 Sacramento St.  415-751-0647 (pamper)
www.marilynjaegerskincare.com
Owner: Marilyn Jaeger

A friendly haven of pampering and beauty, MJS ensures that your experience is unparalleled. Jaeger's philosophy embraces consistency, attentiveness, and beauty in all of its uniqueness. Every dedicated esthetician is trained in her meticulous style, which is reflected in their incomparable treatments, each designed to promote healthy body, spirit, and skin.

## 11. Mom's The Word

3385 Sacramento St.  415-441-8261 (maternity)
www.shop2bmom.com  - Owner: Sarah Pollak

Don't compromise your style for nine months! Let the friendly, knowledgeable women of Mom's the Word dress you in the style to which you are accustomed, even if you are expecting. The fashion conscious pros will outfit you for work, weekend, and special occasions. Mom's extensive collection of styles will astound you. Check out the selection of 7 for All Mankind, Michael Stars, Velvet, and DVF.

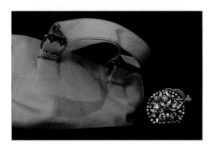

## 12. Nicolette

3375 Sacramento St.  415-563-5400 (boutique)
Owner: Nicole Whitty

Nicolette is a trendy upscale boutique in beautiful Laurel Village. The shop carries everything from fashion-forward lines such as Mason, Milly, and Alice & Olivia to your classic pieces from Theory, Vince, and many more. If you're looking for a boutique that's classic with an edgy twist, then this is the place for you.

Bettina

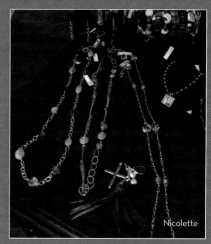

Nicolette

Marilyn Jaeger

Choisis

3loomers

Beau

## Jorja Gaskins

### JORJA

2015 Chestnut St.
415-674-1131

"One of my close girlfriends and I had talked about opening a store for a few years, but what really made it clear to me was the day I went to look for my first black tie dress. I looked everywhere to find a dress and couldn't find one. By the end of day it was clear to me that San Francisco clearly needed a dress store!"

### HOW MUCH MONEY DID IT TAKE TO START?

It's been a long time now, but I think we started with $120,000.

### ADVICE I WOULD GIVE TO WOMEN STARTING THEIR OWN BUSINESS:

Make sure you are passionate about what you're doing. There are going to be days when you love every minute of it, and there are going to be days you don't, but you still have to go to work and have a good attitude because if you don't no one else will.

### MISTAKE THAT I HOPE NOT TO REPEAT:

Thinking you can do everything yourself!

### WHAT I LIKE MOST ABOUT OWNING A BUSINESS:

I love being my own boss. You are responsible for your success and your failures.

### WHAT I LIKE LEAST ABOUT OWNING A BUSINESS:

Not being able to leave your work at the office.

### PEOPLE WOULD BE SURPRISED THAT I.

Still love board games.

### FAVORITE GUILTY PLEASURE SHOPPING:

Any Jimmy Choo Store.

### PERSONAL TIME OFF INDULGENCE:

A warm destination with a great spa!

### 3. Pumpkin, Hip Clothes for Cool Babes

3366 Sacramento St. 415-567-6780 (kids)
www.pumpkinbabes.com - Owner: Alanna Klein
Pumpkin has baby, boys, and girls clothing you
won't find anywhere else. Hip styles and unique
brands make kids look cooler than their parents.
The staff is eager to help with all your shopping
requests in person, by phone, or e-mail. Your kids
will have so much fun shopping at Pumpkin, they
won't want to leave and neither will you.

### 4. Red Dot

76 Chestnut St. 415-346-0606 (boutique)
www.reddotshops.com - Owner: Melissa McLane
Red Dot ferrets out unique, affordable fashion
that's so cute you'll start showing up at the store
on shipment days and so fun you'll bring all your
friends with you for a shopping party. Buyers hunt
down great basics, unique novelty pieces, and
cool little gift items. The shop stocks the kind of
merchandise that you'll want in every color.

### 5. Sarah Shaw

3495 Sacramento St. 415-929-2990 (boutique)
www.sarahshaw.com - Owner: Sarah Shaw
Sarah knows that your home is your refuge from
the outside world. Owner Sarah Shaw's mission
is to provide beautiful and practical products to
make your nest comfortable, welcoming, and delightful. She designs and collaborates with manu-
facturers, both local and international, to bring
you interesting, unique accessories to make your
nest everything you want it to be and more.

### 6. Smash Shoes

2030 Chestnut St. 415-673-4736 (shoes)
-Owner: Genny Lee
This contemporary designer shoe store carries
collections from high-end labels such as Sergio
Rossi, Barbara Bui, and Sigerson Morrison, as well
as sporty lifestyle brands like Puma, Asics, and Nike.
Whether it is elegant sandals, sleek boots, or funky
sneakers, the owners strive to provide the most
intriguing offerings to a clientele with a refined and
acute fashion taste. That's you!

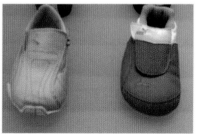

### 17. Soirée San Francisco
2998 Washington St.  415-447-9771 (gifts)
www.soireesanfrancisco.com
Owners: Kathy Swindle & Misty Mueller
Soirée San Francisco is the savvy source for
the latest styles in stationery, invitations, and
announcements. Whether your taste is simple,
sophisticated, or playful, Soirée San Francisco will
guide you in choosing your personalized look.

### 18. Sonoma Country Store
3575 Sacramento St.  415-923-1600 (gifts)
www.sonomacountrystore.com
Owner: Anne Thornton
The Sonoma Country Store carries personal accessories, body products, and home décor. Find
discount pricing for Eileen West in a boutique
atmosphere with gifts and decorating ideas.
Walk through the store, sit on the jasmine-scent-
ed back patio, and decide whether to get that
beautiful scarf for your friend or that soft, warm
throw for your bed...or maybe both.

### 19. Sue Fisher King
3067 Sacramento St.  415-922-7276 (gifts)
www.suefisherking.com - Owner: Sue Fisher King
Home fashion mavens have this store on speed
dial and you should, too. Gorgeous sheets,
fluffy towels, stunning dishes, and table wares
are just a few of the items that lure repeat
visitors. The decorative pillow collection is
unmatched, and you can find a charming gift
at a great price, always wrapped in the shop's
glamorous satin ribbon.

### 20. Tre Balm
3225 Sacramento St.  415-292-5129 (pamper)
www.trebalm.com - Owner: Tracy Cook
Tre Balm is a European boutique and spa that
offers an exquisite collection of exclusive skin
care lines, exotic perfumes, elegant hostess
gifts, make-up, and stylish jewelry and handbags. Complementing its beautiful retail store
is a discreet skin care studio that offers cutting
edge treatments, including hyperbaric oxygen
facials, peels, waxing, and maquillage services.

Two Skirts

Tre Balm

Sonoma Country Store

SMASH

Smash

Red Dot

Moms the Word

## INSPIRATION/MOTIVATION FOR START-ING MY BUSINESS:

It is something that I've always wanted to do, and when my youngest daughter left fo college I knew the moment was at hand!

## HOW MUCH MONEY DID IT TAKE TO START?

A lot! I bought an existing business, which included all of the inventory.

## MISTAKE THAT I HOPE NOT TO REPEAT

I got so excited during my first buying trip, totally overbought.

## WHAT I LIKE MOST ABOUT OWNING A BUSINESS:

The independence it affords me as well as the opportunity to be creative.

## WHAT I LIKE LEAST ABOUT OWNING A BUSINESS:

Worry, worry, worry.

## PEOPLE WOULD BE SURPRISED THAT

Have absolutely no retail experience what so ever, except as a consumer.

## FAVORITE GUILTY PLEASURE SHOP-PING:

Urban Outfitters with my teenage daught

## PERSONAL TIME OFF INDULGENCE:

Facials, manis & pedis, and cooking!

## Maria Muzio

DIVINE GIRLS

340 Presidio Ave.
415-409-4901
www.divinegirls.net

"You should do all of the research and homework that is necessary. But, in the end make sure that your business is a reflection of you and what you want it to be."

## 21. Two Skirts

2124 Chestnut St.  415-441-6727 (boutique)
www.twoskirts.net - Owner: Amanda Corzine
Prepare to discover unique yet classic pieces
that you won't find elsewhere at this sophisticated women's boutique. A high tin ceiling,
chandeliers, and plush dressing rooms provide a
perfect setting for an equally stunning selection
of cocktail dresses and casual wear. Also browse
fabulous handbags by Isabella Fiore and Kisim,
as well as a wide variety of local jewelry designs.

Notes:

# RUSSIAN HILL/POLK STREET

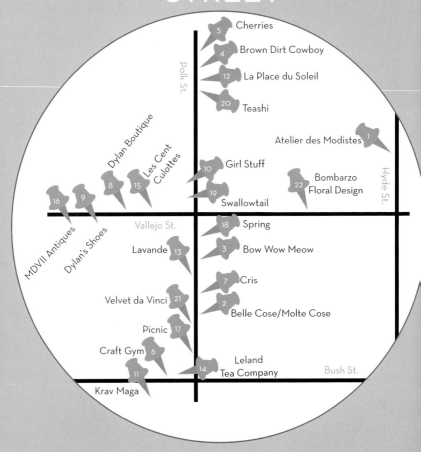

Polk St.

5 Cherries

4 Brown Dirt Cowboy

12 La Place du Soleil

20 Teashi

Hyde St.

1 Atelier des Modistes

Dylan Boutique

Les Cent Culottes

8    15

10 Girl Stuff

22 Bombarzo Floral Design

16   9

19 Swallowtail

MDVII Antiques

Dylan's Shoes

Vallejo St.

18 Spring

Lavande 13

3 Bow Wow Meow

7 Cris

Velvet da Vinci 21

2 Belle Cose/Molte Cose

Picnic 17

Craft Gym 6

11

14 Leland Tea Company

Bush St.

Krav Maga

1. Atelier des Modistes  2. Bella Cose, Molte Cose
3. Bow Wow Meow  4. Brown Dirt Cowboy
5. Cherries  6. Craft Gym  7. Cris  8. Dylan Boutique  9. Dylan Shoes
10. Girl Stuff  11. Krav Maga Training Center  12. La Place du Soleil  13. Lavande
14. Leland Tea Company  15. Les Cent Culottes  16. MDVII Antiques  17. Picnic
18. Spring  19. Swallowtail  20. Teashi  21. Velvet da Vinci

*Don't let the abundance of antique & second hand stores fool you ---- this charming neighborhood sports some of the most exclusive and unusual stores in the City. Take a breather with a pal or your pup at a local bistro and savor this area's European feel.*

### 1. Atelier des Modistes
1903 Hyde St.  415-775-0545 (bridal)
www.atelierdesmodistes.com
Co-owner: Suzanne Hanley
The enchanting Atelier des Modistes features custom wedding gowns and couture designs from co-owner Hanley that begin with luxurious fabrics, and incorporate vintage French trims and gem beading. Each garment is made with uncommon precision and attention to detail. Atelier des Modistes also offers elegant jewelry and unconventional weddings rings.

### 2. Belle Cose, Molte Cose
2036, 2044 Polk St.  415-921-5374 (boutique)
Owner: Teresa Nittolo
Italian for "many things," Molte Cose is aptly named. Opened in 1990 by designer Teresa Nittolo, the shop features new and vintage furniture, decorative objects, jewelry, clothing, and children goods. Second store Belle Cose carries lingerie, apparel, shoes, and accessories. With Molte Cose for men rounding things out, the three connecting stores offer modern haberdashery for all.

### 3. Bow Wow Meow
2150 Polk St.  415-440-2845 (pets)
www.bowwowmeow.net - Manager: Amy Bearg
Awarded "Best Pet Store 2005" and "Best Pet Groomer 2006" by SF Weekly, this is the place to go for all your pets' needs or to pick up a great gift for any pet lover. Bow Wow Meow is one fun store to experience and everything pet- and people-related—kibble, cashmere sweaters, people clothes, beds and bags, bakery treats—is here.

### 4. Brown Dirt Cowboy
2406 Polk Street  415-922-9065 (boutique)
www.browndirtcowboys.com - Owner: Syliva O
In business for 13 years, Brown Dirt Cowboy is a lifestyle design shop, designing and building custom classic and vintage-inspired furniture. The shop stocks an array of complimentary French and American home furnishings, as well as clothing and accessories for the girl who has her own style and wants to add to it.

## INSPIRATION/MOTIVATION FOR STARTING MY OWN BUSINESS:

Wanted to find a way to make a living doing something creative.

## HOW MUCH MONEY DID IT TAKE TO START?

About $25,000.

## MISTAKE THAT I HOPE NOT TO REPEAT:

Getting impatient with my stock and subsequently over buying.

## WHAT I LIKE MOST ABOUT OWNING A BUSINESS:

Creative exchange with my clients.

## WHAT I LIKE LEAST ABOUT OWNING A BUSINESS:

Too much paperwork + 100% responsibility.

## PEOPLE WOULD BE SURPRISED THAT I...

Had no real plan whatsoever.

## FAVORITE GUILTY PLEASURE SHOPPING:

Any second hand store.

## PERSONAL TIME OFF INDULGENCE:

Reading and coming up with my next plan...

### Sylvia Ortiz

BROWN DIRT COWBOY

2406 Polk Street
415-922-9065
www.browndirtcowboys.com

"Hold on to your own identity and don't get caught up in the latest craze – it will soon pass and take all the followers with it."

## Gail Foland

### KRAV MAGA TRAINING CENTER

1455 Bush Street
415-921-0612
www.kravmaga-sf.com

*"We offer you a place to work off that stress, get fit, have fun, and learn real self-defense in a supportive environment."*

### INSPIRATION/MOTIVATION FOR STARTING MY BUSINESS:

I had just recently sold my share of another business and then had started taking Krav Maga classes to get in shape and to lose weight. The main reason why I wanted to get shape was for my brother's wedding, where I was going to be a bridesmaid with women 25 years younger and who all wore size 2. In a relatively short period of time, I lost 40 pounds and got in the best shape of my life at age 50. Since then, I wanted to share with everyone how fun Krav Maga made it to get fit and learn how to defend yourself.

### HOW MUCH MONEY DID IT TAKE TO START?

The total cost of renting our current space, improvements and an opening advertising campaign was about $150,000.

### MY ROLE MODEL:

My role model was my father who owned a tire store and turned that 1 store into a chain of over 30 stores in 2 states with wholesale centers that covered 4 states. He worked hard for over 40 years and definitely had his ups and downs in business, but learned from every mistake as well as every success.

### ADVICE I WOULD GIVE TO WOMEN STARTING THEIR OWN BUSINESS:

Start by following your passion – Pick your investors and partners very carefully, it's easier to get a divorce than get rid of a business partner. Have a business plan and at least 25% more capital than you think you will need. Be prepared to work long hours. Be creative with marketing ideas. Get involved in the community, and network, network, network.

### WHAT I LIKE MOST ABOUT OWNING A BUSINESS:

Working with the public.

## 5. Cherries

2436 Polk St.  415-441-0310 (flowers)
www.cherriesflowers.com
Owners: Katherine Oliver & Kimberly Engle
Open since 2001, Cherries has garnered a loyal
following of San Franciscans who have a taste for
Victorian romance. Owners Oliver and Engle are
classic and careful in their selection of flowers and
vintage containers. Cherries offers complimentary
consultations for weddings and events. Floral gift
deliveries are made daily and can be contracted
by phone.

## 6. Craft Gym

1452 Bush St.   415-441-6223 (gifts)
www.craftgym.com
Owners: Jackie Ortega & Jane Logan
Both novice and experienced do-it-yourself types
flock to this hip studio for workshops, private
lessons, and space to start, store, and finish their
own creations. Craft Gym offers access to equipment and quality instruction in jewelry, sewing,
knitting, ceramics, metals, paper, textiles, and
more. By providing supplies for all workshops and
events, Craft Gym makes it easy to exercise your
creativity.

## 7. Cris

2056 Polk St.  415-474-1191 (boutique)
Owner: Cris Zander
For 15 years, this consignment boutique has ca-
tered to women with champagne tastes, carrying
current ready-to-wear styles from Chanel, Prada,
Cocca, Hermes, Dolce & Gabbana, Comme des
Garcons, as well as American sportswear designers. A native of Milan, former designer Zander
looks for clothes in excellent condition, and some
even feature original price tags. Purchases are
packaged with raffia and dried flowers.

## 8. Dylan Boutique

506 Vallejo St.  415-931-8721 (boutique)
www.dylanboutique.com - Owner: Stephanie Unger
This boutique is for serious style-seekers, carrying
coveted denim from Superfine, Acne, and more;
fashion-plate favorites by Jill Stuart, Sue Stemp
and their ilk; and of the moment aussie labels:
Ksubi, Lover, and Sass & Bide. A day at Dylan feels
like going shopping in your best friend's closet...
if your best friend were Kate Moss that is. Fun accessories like headbands, hats and gloves.

## 9. Dylan Shoes

1507 Vallejo St.  415-931-8721 (shoes)
www.dylanboutique.com - Owner: Stephanie Unger
At Dylan Shoes, retail therapy has new meaning
with a finely tuned selection from lines including:
Chloe, Proenza Schouler, Marc Jacobs Collection, Stella McCartney, and more. You'll find
everything from flip-flops to five-inch heels.

## 10. Girl Stuff

2255 Polk St.  415-409-2426 (boutique)
Owner: Tracy Green
This sweet little jewel box is stocked with of essential goodies for every woman that will keep he
(i.e. you) looking great from head to toe. The sho
also features fabulous children's clothing for little
guys and gals 0-6 years.

## 11. Krav Maga Training Center

1455 Bush St.  415-921-0612 (self-defense)
www.kravmaga-sf.com - Owner: Gail Foland
Bored with running nowhere on the treadmill?
Stressed out? Work off that stress, get fit, have
fun, and learn self defense in a supportive
environment. Krav Maga is a self-defensive and
fitness system that is easy to learn and extremely
effective. The 6,000-square-foot facility features
more than 65 classes, including self defense,
strength training, conditioning, yoga, sparring, an
grappling.

## 12. La Place du Soleil

2356 Polk St.  415-771-4252 (décor)
www.laplacedusoleilsf.com - Owner: Amy Dean
All kinds of goodies lurk within this jewel box of
shop. Antiques, gifts, teas, and European candle
are packaged in original and adorable ways. Own
Amy Dean travels to Europe as often as possible
seeking the rare and unusual, not an easy task in
town filled with great shops.

Belle Cose/Molte Cose

Brown Dirt Cowboy

Cherries

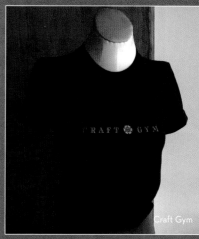
Craft Gym

Dylan's Shoes

Girl Stuff

## Stephanie Unger

DYLAN BOUTIQUE AND DYLAN SHOES

1506 Vallejo St. and 1507 Vallejo St.
415-931-8721
www.dylanboutique.com

"In November 2004, we opened Dylan Boutique. In March 2006, we open Dylan Shoes across the street... We work to bring you the best of ready to wear international fashion tailored to the unique style of today's San Franciscans. New York and Los Angeles should not be the only cities in the U.S. where people feel they can find the forward fashion they are looking for."

**MY ROLE MODEL/MENTOR:**
Estee Lauder is probably the most inspirational businesswoman for me. Her empire started based on her desire to make women feel good about themselves and feel beautiful, and because her principles come from a true love of what her business is about and represents, more so than a profit margin, her empire continues to be one of the most successful ever created by a woman.

**ADVICE I WOULD GIVE TO WOMEN STARTING THEIR OWN BUSINESS:**
Do what you know, not just what you love. It's okay to learn computer programs, and easier procedural strategies in order to pursue opening up a business you love, but it's going to be more work than reward if you decide to go into something that isn't second nature.

**MISTAKE THAT I HOPE NOT TO REPEAT**
Hiring without a trial period.

**WHAT I LIKE MOST ABOUT OWNING A BUSINESS:**
I love seeing women leave the store feeling beautiful and good about themselves.

**WHAT I LIKE LEAST ABOUT OWNING A BUSINESS:**
The pressure to make the 'right' decisions for your business. It's enough to keep you up every night.

**PEOPLE WOULD BE SURPRISED THAT**
Used to, and often still, freelance as a field producer for MTV.

**FAVORITE GUILTY PLEASURE SHOPPING PLACE:**
Sephora. I'm a closet product junkie.

**PERSONAL TIME OFF INDULGENCE:**
Reading my stack of WWDs while getting a pedi.

### 13. Lavande

2139B Polk St.  415-931-7389 (pamper)
www.lavandenailspa.com-Owner: Stephanie Leung
Lavande Nail Spa was created with the vision
that everyone deserves to be pampered without
breaking the bank. You no longer have to suffer
the high price of a day spa or the low quality of a
discount nail salon. Treatments combine plant and
flower essences and indigenous herbs with traditional spa services for maximum healing results.
Drop in and indulge in a getaway experience.

### 14. Leland Tea Company

416 Bush St.  415-346-4832 (tea)
www.lelandtea.com - Manager: Carmen Ortiz
Cast aside those associations with musty cozies
and chipped china—Leland Tea Company is proof
that tea drinking doesn't have to be stuffy, pokey,
or precious. Owner Ortiz encourages visitors to
browse, sniff the teas and the scent of baking
scones, mix their own unique tea cocktails, and
relax or surf the Internet via the free Wi-Fi zone.

### 15. Les Cent Culottes

504 Vallejo St.  415-614-2586 (lingerie)
www.lescentculottes.com-Owner: Sophie Baudet
Owner Sophie Baudet provides an intimate
atmosphere and confidence to her clientele in
his delightful little lingerie store. Whether you
are seeking personal lingerie or a special gift, it
is guaranteed to have high quality and beauty.
The elegant, well-made, and oh-so delicate bras
(from 32A to 38DD), panties, boxers thongs,
garters, nightwear, and bustiers are all imported
from France.

### 16. MDVII Antiques

507 1/2 Vallejo St.  415-931-4213 (boutique)
Owner: Susie Hoimes
MDVII is a charming antique shop in fashionable
Russian Hill. Owner Hoimes is British, Kenya-born
daughter of an old colonialist, who blends her
extreme international style with a deep English
knowledge of the world's finest and most unique
artifacts. Her specialties are vintage costume and
fine jewelry, Venetian glass, and antiques. This
shop is a true San Francisco jewel.

### 17. Picnic

1808 Polk St.  415-346-6556 (boutique)
www.picnicsf.com - Owner: Jasmine Tan
Step inside this darling boutique and you're sure
to find some pretty item at every turn. With a
cool vintage, flea-market vibe, Picnic stocks lovely
frocks, cool tees, luscious candles for your home,
and everything else in between. So drop by and
pick something up pretty and perk up your mood
in the process.

### 18. Spring

2162 Polk St.  415-673-2065 (décor)
www.astorecalledspring.com
Manager: Wendi Goad
Spring is a specialty retail store specializing in
green products for a healthy home. The shop aims
to improve the air quality in homes by reducing
exposure to chemicals, toxins, and pollutants (for
the benefit of personal health and the environment). Spring is for anyone who wishes to manage
her home in a greener, safer, and healthier way.

### 19. Swallowtail

2217 Polk St.  415-567-1555 (décor)
www.swallowtailsf.com
Owner: Sheri Sheridan
This gallery specializes in classic antiques and
quirky, vintage collectibles designed to give your
home a distinct flare. The moody, atrium-like space
transports shoppers to another era—from paintings, prints, and photography by local artists, cus-
tom-upholstered settees and Louis XV armchairs
to Lucite side tables and one-of-a-kind objets d'art,
a wealth of treasures await you at Swallowtail.

### 20. Teashi

2340 Polk St.  415-749-0990 (pamper)
www.teashi.com - Manager: Noni Onossian
This hip day spa offers a chic, open space filled
with details like pink toile and porcelain pedicure tubs. Known for its expert nail services,
facials, waxing, and massages, Teashi pampers
you while you sip on tea, listen to cool tunes,
and trust that sanitation and environmental
friendliness is a focus.

Teashi

Spring

os Cent Culottes

Leland Tea Co.

ris

Dylan Boutique

## INSPIRATION/MOTIVATION FOR START-ING MY BUSINESS:

This would have to be my mom. She is a very wise and strong woman who has always been supportive of my ventures and dreams. She's inspired me from childhood, when she used to design and sew my clothing. This lead to my interests in fashion and design.

## HOW MUCH MONEY DID IT TAKE TO START?

Definitely not enough.

## MY ROLE MODELS/MENTORS:

I would have to say my sisters and brother – they have all played a part, and are involved in their own businesses, or have strong positions in their field of employment. They have always encouraged me.

## ADVICE I WOULD GIVE TO WOMEN STARTING THEIR OWN BUSINESS:

Be prepared to work hard. It takes lots of devotion and time to run a business. Surround yourself with supportive people who believe in you. Do not expect instant results.

## WHAT I LIKE MOST ABOUT OWNING A BUSINESS:

I love the creative freedom and the people you meet – they are the ones that keep you going.

## WHAT I LIKE LEAST ABOUT OWNING A BUSINESS:

At times, I wish it were a little easier... Retail is very up and down. A little more consistency would be nice.

## PEOPLE WOULD BE SURPRISED THAT

I am obsessed with Animal Planet. It is one of my favorite TV shows. I fantasize about safaris, traveling around, studying and helping animals.

# Theresa Nittolo

### BELLE COSE/MOLTE COSE

2036 & 2044 Polk Street
415-921-5374
415-474-3494

"When in doubt, don't do it. Follow your instincts and your dreams."

## 21. Velvet da Vinci

2015 Polk St.  415-441-0109 (boutique)
www.velevetdavinci.com
Co-Owner: Elizabeth Shypertt

Beautiful pieces of true art that you can wear or display in your home are what you'll find at Velvet da Vinci. All of the work is made in studios by the artists themselves. Find jewelry and sculpture from around the world that is modern, museum-quality, and one of a kind. Don't wait for that "special someone" to buy yourself the fabulous jewelry you want.

Notes:

# UNION SQUARE/MAIDEN LANE/DOWNTOWN

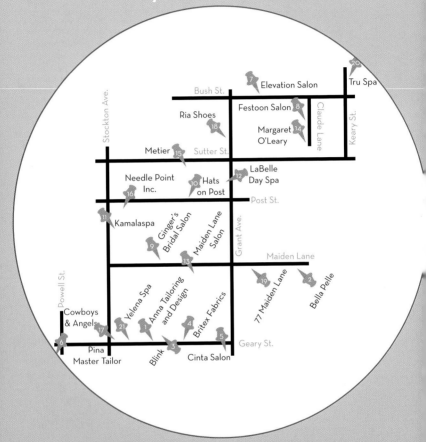

1. Anna Tailoring & Design  2. Bella Pellé Skin Studio

3. Blink Eyebrows & Cosmetics  4. Britex Fabrics  5. Cinta Salon

6. Cowboys and Angels  7. Elevation Salon & Café  8. Festoon Salon

9. Ginger's Bridal Salon  10. Hats on Post  11. Kamalaspa & Salon

12. LaBelle Day Spa and Salon  13. Maiden Lane Salon  14. Margaret O'Leary

15. Metier  16. Needlepoint, Inc.  17. Pina Master Tailor  18. Ria Shoes

19. 77 Maiden Lane Salon & Spa  20. Tru  21. Yelena Spa

Locals know there's more to this swanky shopping mecca than mere chain stores and upscale boutiques. Tool down the many alleys & side streets to refuel with yummy eats at Parisian-style outdoor cafes for a post purchase treat!

### 1. Anna Tailoring & Design

166 Geary St, Suite 503  415-391-6868 (sewing)
Owner: Anna Lishansky

If you need any item altered or custom designed, take it to the place with more than 30 years of experience in both European and American tailoring: Anna Tailoring and Design. Not only does Anna work with a private clientele, she also works with high-end boutiques such as Yves Saint Laurent, Prada, Hermes, Max Mara, and Neiman Marcus.

### 2. Bella Pellé Skin Studio

9 Maiden Lane  415-362-6384 (pamper)
www.bellapelle.com - Owner: Shelley Costantini

In-the-know beauties dash to BellaPellé Skin Studio for gorgeous skin, glamorous beauty extras, and sinfully sexy waxing. Stylish beauties particularly swoon for our custom-blended mineral make-up and lush lash extensions. A sophisticated setting and a friendly, dedicated staff whose goal is to uncover one's most exquisite "bella pellé" (Italian for "beautiful skin") make for fabulous results and fun beauty experience.

### 3. Blink Eyebrows & Cosmetics

166 Geary St., Ste. 1305–415-399-0789 (pamper)
www.blinksf.com - Owner: Anna Lee

Specializing exclusively in face artistry, Blink focuses on enhancing brows, lashes and makeup appearance. Each appointment is booked in a timely manner and meticulously performed by makeup artists. Eyebrows are shaped and structured only by tweezing, trimming, and threading, never with wax. All lash extensions and tints are done with high-quality products. Skin is threaded with the softest cotton string from Asia.

### 4. Britex Fabrics

146 Geary St.  415-392-2910 (sewing)
www.britexfabrics.com
Owners: Lucy, Beverly, & Sharman Spector

Fabric, buttons, and bridal, oh my! Located in the heart of Union Square since 1952, Britex Fabrics is home to four floors of fabulous fashion, home décor fabrics, more than 30,000 different buttons, yarns, faux flowers, countless ribbons, books, trims, beads, and, yep, feathers. Close your eyes and repeat after us: "There's no place like Britex...There's no place like Britex..."

**INSPIRATION/MOTIVATION FOR START-
ING MY BUSINESS:**

My husband and I sold our tire business
and I wanted to do something else.

**HOW MUCH MONEY DID IT TAKE TO
START?**

A lot!

**MY ROLE MODELS/MENTORS:**

My father and my husband.

**ADVICE I WOULD GIVE TO WOMEN
STARTING THEIR OWN BUSINESS:**

Plan on double the money you think you
will spend. Have a back up plan.

**MISTAKE THAT I HOPE NOT TO REPEAT:**

Trusting other people to make decisions
for me.

**WHAT I LIKE MOST ABOUT OWNING A
BUSINESS:**

Communication with employees and mostly
all clients.

**WHAT I LIKE LEAST ABOUT OWNING A
BUSINESS:**

The bad manners of both employees and
clients.

**FAVORITE GUILTY PLEASURE SHOP-
PING:**

Neiman Marcus.

**PERSONAL TIME OFF INDULGENCE:**

Relaxing and reading.

## Sherlee Rhine

77 MAIDEN LANE SALON & SPA

77 Maiden Lane, 2nd Floor
415-391-7777
www.77maidenlane.com

*"I love to come to work
every day."*

## Sheri Evans

METIER

355 Sutter St.
415-989-5395
www.metiersf.com

"I adore fashion and good design and
find them endlessly inspiring. At a very
young age I decided I wanted to have
my own store — I was the kid who added
to her outfit on the way to school from a
stash I kept hidden near the bus stop."

**HOW MUCH MONEY DID IT TAKE TO START?**
$60,000.

**MY ROLE MODELS/MENTORS:**
My mother and grandmother were my role models; they were always so chic. My father was my mentor and I looked to him because he'd been running his own business since he was 20.

**ADVICE I WOULD GIVE TO WOMEN STARTING THEIR OWN BUSINESS:**
Do it because you love it and treat your staff as best you can within your means.

**MISTAKE THAT I HOPE NOT TO REPEAT:**
Don't lose your focus or spread yourself too thin. When I started, I had women's, men's, accessories, and home furnishings. I spent too much money on inventory and it wasn't clear who my market was.

**WHAT I LIKE MOST ABOUT OWNING A BUSINESS:**
Making the decisions.

**WHAT I LIKE LEAST ABOUT OWNING A BUSINESS:**
Making the decisions.

**PEOPLE WOULD BE SURPRISED THAT I.**
Have a husband who doesn't care about fashion.

**FAVORITE GUILTY PLEASURE SHOPPING**
Target.

**PERSONAL TIME OFF INDULGENCE:**
Calistoga mud baths

## 5. Cinta Salon

23 Grant Ave., 2nd Floor  415-989-1000 (pamper)
www.cinta.com - Owner: Cinta Gibbons
Cinta Salon, an urban beauty retreat in the heart
of San Francisco's Union Square, is a full-service
destination offering hair, spa, nail, and make-up
services. In the 4,000-square-feet loft, creativity flows as clients and stylists interact. Whether
you're looking for an outrageous change or
a simple cleanup, Cinta Salon's highly skilled
professionals will tailor their fresh, cutting-edge
techniques to fit your style.

## 6. Cowboys and Angels

207 Powell St., Suite 400  415-362-8516 (pamper)
www.cowboysandangelssf.com
Co-Owners: Louise Baranowski & Tracey McAlister
This downtown salon features high ceilings and
industrial flooring, and is filled with light, art, and
music. The art is a rotating exhibit, the music a mix
of current sound, and the view from the windows
provides an ever-changing urban landscape. Four
stories above Union Square, stylists work to reinvent what has been, with their fingers on the pulse
of what's to come.

## 7. Elevation Salon & Café

451 Bush St.  415-392-2969 (pamper)
www.elevationsalon.com-Manager: Jody McCallum
Elevation Salon has become the setting for hair
and couture fashion shows, as well as other
events. The salon's artistic team sets trends twice
a year with spring/summer and fall/winter fore-
casts. In-house seminars and training, as well as at-
tending hair and fashion events here and abroad,
ensure the stylists stay über-knowledgeable and
on the cutting edge.

## 8. Festoon Salon

Claude Lane  888-357-2566 (pamper)
www.festoonsalon.com - Owner: Melissa Ryan
Voted best hair salon by Citysearch and the
East Bay Express, Festoon Salon is the place
to get beautified. Expert stylists and stylists-in-
training make this salon accessible for everyone
in the Bay Area. Devotees to Bumble and
bumble will find the full product line, including
the exclusive Treatment line, in both salons.

## 9. Ginger's Bridal Salon
130 Maiden Lane, Ste. M100  415-781-8559 (bridal)
www.gingers-sf.com
Owners: Ivana Ristic & Lynn Rosenzweig
Ginger's carries timeless, modern designer wedding gowns, including Ristarose couture. This Maiden Lane salon is elegant and you'll be guided and assisted by a savvy sales staff. Prices range from $2,500–$7,500. By appointment only.

## 10. Hats on Post
210 Post St., Suite 606  415-392-3737 (boutique)
Owner: Sheryl Krajewski
Hats on Post is a small—you guessed it—hat shop brimming with hats, whether it's for fun in the sun or cold weather. There is an assortment of whimsical and outrageous hats and, of course, basic, classical styles. Top off an outfit with a beautiful chapeau from Hats on Post.

## 11. Kamalaspa & Salon
240 Stockton St., 7th Floor  415-217-7700 (pamper
www.kamalaspa.com
Co-owner: Amber Marie Bently
Inspired by the Raj era of East India, Kamalaspa & Salon is designed to resemble a Maharaja's tent. Located right on Union Square, the spa focuses on Ayurvedic treatments, including the Abhyanga or four-hand massage, and Shirodhara. The spa also offers nail and salon services, reiki, traditiona Swedish massage, and shiatsu.

## 12. LaBelle Day Spa and Salon
233 Grant Ave.  415-433-7644 (pamper)
www.LaBelleDaySpas.com
Owner: Bella Schneider
LaBelle Day Spa & Salon is a three- floor oasis of quiet luxury in the heart of downtown San Francisco. Its full-service menu includes clinical and anti-aging skin care, endermologie, massage, expert nail care, hair dressing and makeup. Relax in front of a fireplace and enjoy a complimentary foot treatment while luxuriating in LaBelle's stylis European décor.

Margaret O'Leary

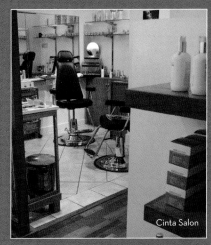

Cinta Salon

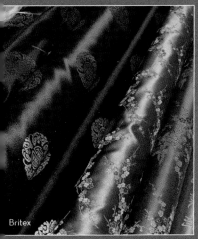

Britex

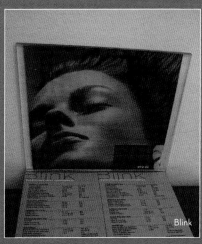

Blink

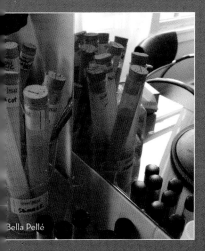

Bella Pellé

Cowboys & Angels

## INSPIRATION/MOTIVATION FOR STARTING MY BUSINESS:

For over 20 years, I helped many clients to feel beautiful. I realized there is an endless passion I have for this industry. I guess it was all the faces that I worked on inspired me. Behind each face, I could somehow make a difference in their lives.

## HOW MUCH MONEY DID IT TAKE TO START?

Roughly around $80,000.

## ADVICE I WOULD GIVE TO WOMEN STARTING THEIR OWN BUSINESS

Treat each client as the last and only client you have that day. Go above and beyond to understand each individual's need. Be passionate about what you're gifted at and make it exciting. Also, be generous and loving towards your employees. It will show great harmony and energy through out the day.

## MISTAKE THAT I HOPE NOT TO REPEAT

I hope not to overbook my schedule severely to the point that I would jeopardize my health and become ill. In order for me to take care of others, I have to learn to stay and healthy consistently.

## WHAT I LIKE MOST ABOUT OWNING A BUSINESS:

It is most rewarding to see my team grow and blossom. I started from one artist to four. They all built rapidly and became very busy. I like to see new clients leave happy and comment on their fine work.

## WHAT I LIKE LEAST ABOUT OWNING A BUSINESS:

I am more an artist and educator. I don't enjoy bookkeeping, inventory and payroll. But taking care of numbers and operation part of being a small business owner.

## Anna Lee

BLINK EYEBROWS AND COSMETICS

166 Geary St.
415-399-0789
www.blinksf.com

"It's tough being a female business owner. Always stay calm and focus. It's o.k. to make mistakes. Learn from it and move on."

## 13. Maiden Lane Salon

11 Maiden Lane  415-981-2426 (pamper)
www.maidenlanesalon.com
Owner: Lena Tulchinsky

Maiden Lane Salon was established more 10 years
ago in the heart of Union Square. With comfort
and quality as the focus, the salon features some
of the Bay Area's top designers and is convenient-
ly located near world-famous hotels, restaurants,
and boutiques. The full-service salon provides hair
services and treatments, plus a choice of body
and beauty therapies.

## 14. Margaret O'Leary

One Claude Lane  415-391-1010 (boutique)
www.margaretoleary.com  - Manager: Teresa O'Leary
Specializing in laid-back feminine knitwear, this
boutique's label attracts stars—including Jennifer
Garner, Reese Witherspoon, Marcia Cross, and
Madonna—who can't get enough of the super-soft
cashmere sweaters. The Fillmore Street location
also carries a selection of West Coast collections,
including Stewart+Brown's sustainable-fabric
basics, Robindira Unsworth's neohippie jewelry,
and Calleen Cordero's footwear.

## 15. Metier

355 Sutter St.  415-989-5395 (boutique)
www.metiersf.com - Owner: Sheri Evans
Every season Sheri Evans selects the most
seductive pieces by designers who share her
preference for distinctive silhouettes. Metier's
sartorial mix—featuring Mayle, 3.1 Phillip Lim,
Daryl K, and Blumarine—consistently attracts
women who love beautifully crafted clothes.
The shop also carries jewelry: contemporary
artists Cathy Waterman, 10 Thousand Things,
and Philip Crangi.

## 16. Needlepoint, Inc.

275 Post St., 2nd Floor  415-392-1622 (sewing)
www.needlepointinc.com  - Owner: Diane Nerheim
Discover one of the world's largest and most
complete needlepoint stores. Needlepoint, Inc. is a
designer, retailer, and finisher of fine needlepoint.
Shoppers will find every color and fiber used in
needlepoint, including the shop's line of 100-per-
cent Chinese silk (in 476 vivid colors). Free lessons
are a part of the Needlepoint, Inc. shopping
experience.

### 17. Pina Master Tailor
166 Geary St., Suite 502  415-397-2450 (sewing)
Owner/Master Tailor: Pina Caltagirone
Share and create your dreams through Pina's gifted hands. Pina sewed dresses for herself as a little girl in Sicily, Italy, before she and her sisters attended a school of arts to master needle and thread. Pina has shared her joy of clothing with the Bay Area for more than 40 years. Take your time and surrender to Pina's charm.

### 18. Ria Shoes
301 Grant Ave.  415-834-1420 (shoes)
Owner: Ria Lameraner
If you are looking for comfortable shoes with a flare, visit Ria Shoes at the corner of Grant Avenue and Sutter Street. Since 1968, Ria has provided a great selection of styles, ranging from casual to dress, from vendors such as Ecco, Dansko, Rieker, Merrill, Mephisto, Arche, and Think, just to name a few.

### 19. 77 Maiden Lane Salon & Spa
77 Maiden Lane, 2nd Floor  415-391-7777 (pamper)
www.77maidenlane.com - Owner: Sherlee Rhine
In business for 21 years, this salon and spa enjoys a 10,000-square-foot space with views of Maiden Lane and Grant Avenue. It offers an exhilarating personal experience for both men and women, with the theory that the surroundings should complement the client. This full-service salon and spa is open seven days a week.

### 20. Tru
750 Kearny St.  415-399-9700 (pamper)
www.truspa.com-Manager: Ania Mankowska-Allard
Tru pioneered the modern "day spa" concept, and this downtown spa boasts a dazzling array of innovations designed to enhance the overall experience. The oxygen facials have been a phenomenon since they opened, and any massage should be followed by a journey to the Tropical Rainforest Room, where steam, rain, and a waterfall will wash your cares away.

Ginger's Bridal

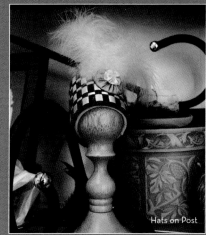

Hats on Post

Kamala Spa

La Belle

Margaret O'Leary

Yelana

## Amber Marie Bently

KAMALASPA & SALON

240 Stockton St., 7th Floor
415-217-7700
www.kamalaspa.com

"*Starting a small business is tough, but very rewarding. It shows that there is more to life than an empty nine-to-five job. Running your own business is like taking financial statements, parties, managers, staff, and a little bit of fun – blending it all together and making a unique cocktail drink!*"

### INSPIRATION/MOTIVATION FOR STARTING MY BUSINESS:
We trekked throughout Rajastan, experienced the beauty of Ayurveda, and brough back our new knowledge to the states

### HOW MUCH MONEY DID IT TAKE TO START?
The build out cost 2.3 million and it took approximately another 1 million to run the business during its first year.

### ADVICE I WOULD GIVE TO WOMEN STARTING THEIR OWN BUSINESS:
Have a lot of capital – because not only to you have to have the build out costs, you have to have enough to pay for the business to keep running until it can sustai itself

### MISTAKE THAT I HOPE NOT TO REPEAT:
Spending too much on print advertisemen

### WHAT I LIKE MOST ABOUT OWNING A BUSINESS:
Being how proud you can be in seeing a success that you created, and of course making my own hours!

### WHAT I LIKE LEAST ABOUT OWNING A BUSINESS:
The stress that you are constantly under during the first two years – whether you ar going to break even or not. And just the responsibility of having so many people to care for.

### PEOPLE WOULD BE SURPRISED THAT I
This is my second business that I have started with my husband, and we used to be starving artists.

### FAVORITE GUILTY PLEASURE SHOPPING:
Buying a little something at Tiffany's or a pair of Manolo Blahnik shoes.

### PERSONAL TIME OFF INDULGENCE:
Definitely massage!

## 21. Yelena Spa

166 Geary St., Suite 1107  415-397-2484 (pamper)
www.yelena-spa.com - Owner: Yelena Blumin
This Union Square day spa is dedicated to
enhancing your appearance, restoring flagging
spirits, and renewing your sense of well being
with personalized beauty services for skin, body,
and nails for both women and men. Enjoy an
indulgent and necessary experience that's offers
a modern take on the European spa tradition.

Notes:

# A SPACE FOR YOUR NOTES

# Index

# A SPACE FOR YOUR NOTES

## BRIDAL

A SPACE FOR YOUR NOTES

# A SPACE FOR YOUR NOTES

# A SPACE FOR YOUR NOTES

# A SPACE FOR YOUR NOTES

## PETS

## PILATES

# A SPACE FOR YOUR NOTES

## TEA

## YOGA

# WOMEN IN THE LIMELIGHT

CRAVE Party!™
What do YOU Crave?
Lotions
Potions
Trinkets
Glitz
Baubles
Plum
Pink
Frocks
And other must-haves.
What more could a girl want?

# CRAVE Party! ™

### What do YOU Crave?

## What is a Crave Party?

A Crave Party is an exclusive, festive, glam-gal gathering of fun, entertainment, personal pampering, specialty shopping, sippin' & noshin' and just hanging with the girls.

### "Everything You Crave" — all under one roof.

Indulge and splurge (you deserve it)
on spa treatments, massages, manis & pedis, fashion shows, irresistible boutique shopping - all in a spirited and carefree atmosphere.

Bring your mom, your best gal-pals, your sisters, daughters, even your bridesmaids! Jump in with both pretty feet and discover what YOU crave!

click: www.craveparty.com
ping: crave@craveparty.com
ring: 206.282.0173

Do you want to be the first to know when the next CRAVE Party is? Sign up for our mailing list and we will keep you in the loop.

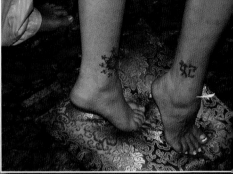

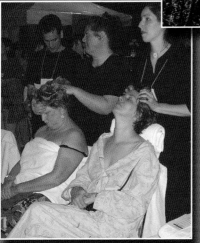

# CRAVE Party!
### What do YOU C

**SUSAN BARNES** *Graphic Designer*

Susan says, "a job where the predominant color is pink?....count me in!! I have found more "must haves" while working on this book than in all the department store mailers combined!" She has been a grahic designer for the past 9 years and specializes i promotional pieces, identity collateral, packaging and invitations Shoot her an email if you have a fun and fabulous project you need help with. When she's not working, you can find her in cyberspace while she lounges on the beach in Thailand. *sbdesign@gmail.com*

**MEGAN MYERS** *CRAVE Maven*

Since starting as an intern at Crave back in June 2005 to taking the reins at Crave events, working for Ladies Who Launch, and helping start up Crave Party in other cities, Megan has a good head for planning fun events. Armed with a Bachelors degree in Communication and a minor in Spanish from Western Washington University, Megan always makes sure everything is in perfect order. In her spare time, Megan also helps plan private events.

**HEIDI LENZE** *Editor*

In the role of Managing Editor – a.k.a. The Book "Lady" (euphemism) at Crave HQ, Heidi Lenze supplied her talents as tas master, content cajoler, and copy-wrangler. Heidi got her start in publishing during a four-year stint in New York and abroad, where she worked in various capacities at a literary agency and briefly at a British tabloid, before being lured back into the comfy womb of Seattle's easy living in 2003. She continues to develop a diverse range of titles + projects offering style and substance – but never simultaneously.

**CARMEN KEIL** *Intern*

Carmen Keil is currently a student at the Art Institute of Seattle With a major in Graphic Design, Carmen is passionate about an artistic outlook on life. Eagerly waiting for graduation, she currently interns for Crave Party and loves her field of choice. Seattle born, she plans to stay and work in her hometown that she loves so much!

**KAYCIE ROBERTS** *photographer*

Kaycie's collaboration with Crave began after participating in a Ladies Who Launch Incubator. Inspired by the idea of working with women entrepreneurs, Kaycie took on the enviable task of photographing some of the most exciting boutiques in the City promote the diverse, women-owned businesses in each unique San Francisco neighborhood. A native of San Francisco, Kaycie has graduate degrees in architecture from Columbia in New York City and in fine art photography from the San Francisco A Institute. www.kaycieroberts.com; kaycie@kaycieroberts.com

Jennifer Worick is the author of more than 15 sassy books, including Girl Group Confidential, Rebound Rituals, and the New York Times bestseller, The Worst-Case Scenario Survival Handbook: Dating & Sex. She lives in Seattle with her impressive shoe collection, makes jewelry and knits in her spare time, and is always on the lookout for the perfect pair of jeans and cocktails that taste like candy. fillyjen@earthlink.net

In 2000, Allie worked at salesforce.com. After 5 years she was ready to take a risk and started her mission to end the unbalance in women's lives by helping them live their entrepreneurial dreams. By leading Ladies Who Launch Incubators she connects like-minded women who are ready to or who have already taken steps towards business success. In her other business, Business Legs, she coaches individuals in the start-up stage and helps busy entrepreneurs network with others. She is passionate about discussing strategies and sorting out the logistics for each unique business to succeed. acovarrubias@ladieswholaunch.com

Amanda Ford is a true urban girl with a passion for film, fashion and food. She is the author of Retail Therapy: Life Lessons Learned While Shopping and her work appeared in numerous publications across the country. When Amanda isn't writing, you can find her perfecting her Lindy Hop skills on the dance floor or escaping the city to blaze trails on her mountain bike. Visit Amanda at her website, www.oholive.com.

Tom Stone was born on a train outside of Mexico City traveling to Puerto Angel, Oaxaca. His parents separated soon after his birth. He grew up with his mother in various communal and nomadic settings in Hawaii and California. He graduated from Harvard University with a degree in Computer Science and worked in Silicon Valley for a number of years in investment banking and in the technology industry. He is a documentary photographer known for his portraits of people living along the edges of society.

Paul discovered his love for photography when he volunteered to help take pictures for the 1st CRAVE Seattle book. He dusted off his 35mm and started shooting. He has since immersed himself in the art of color, emulsions, and has discovered his passion. His talent for capturing the essense of our featured businesses comes naturally. Nicknamed " Dr. Melody" (Melody being the creator of the book) Paul has been around the CRAVE Parties since they originated. rmelody1@hotmail.com

Additional contributors: Evelyn Wong, Anna Forslund

JENNIFER WORICK Writer

ALISON COVARRUBIAS

AMANDA FORD Writer

TOM STONE photographer

PAUL BUTTERFIELD Photographer